My Little Sister

Norma Iris Pagan Morales

ISBN 978-1-959895-86-2 (paperback)
ISBN 978-1-959895-85-5 (ebook)

Printed in the United States of America

Overview

From the tropical paradise of Ponce, Puerto Rico, to the streets of Brooklyn, New York, The Pagan Sisters experienced a Contrast of cultures that are rich and diverse. Norma and Adelin embrace their heritage and come to terms with their love of the Island and life in New York City.

They pay homage to the struggles their parents and siblings faced when they moved from Puerto Rico in search of a better life, that is what their parents thought. It wasn't like that at all.

They didn't have to leave Puerto Rico. Their father had a great job and was also in the Puerto Rico National Guard.

As you read this novel, you will see it is funny, honest, and a lasting bond of two sisters who were always together.

Dedication

This is book is dedicated to my late sister, Adelin Milagros Pagan Morales. She was always there to praise my work. Thank you, sis, for always being so kind. I will never forget you.

Contents

Chapter 1

My Sister

ADELIN MILAGROS PAGAN MORALES

My dear sister Adelin, which I love with all my heart. What can I say about her? Well, like any normal family, we grew up surrounded by lovable parents. My sister is younger than me. We shared everything.

As we got older, we got even closer. We used to talk about boys and friends in general. When it came to choosing a high school, my sister went to the same school I went, Prospect Heights H.S. in Brooklyn, New York.

I used to give her a lot of advice and she did listen. She was a sweet and gentle child. I was the opposite. I guess I was the mother hen to all my siblings.

I recalled one time when a girl came to our block in Brooklyn. She was calling my sister. My parents weren't home. Adelin went downstairs and this girl way older than us wanted to fight. I ran so fast from our apartment to meet this girl.

This young lady came claiming that Adelin was going out with her cousin's boyfriend. I told her to mind her own business. It wasn't my sister fault that the so-called boyfriend didn't want her cousin anymore.

Well, guess what? She came forward to hit my sister. That is when I got so angry that I turned into a lunatic on top of that abnormal girl. I warned her not to get close to my sister. She didn't listen.

In the meantime, the other girls around the block came forward. I told them that I can take care of the situation, but to stand by just in case I needed help.

Adelin just stood there crying. I took a stick and hit both girls. The two girls couldn't fight back. I beat them badly. They were on the ground for a while. I stopped fighting and the girls ran without a word.

When the fight was over, we went to the corner store for some ice cream. The owner gave us free milkshakes because he knew those girls were trouble. The whole block congratulated me, and the two losers went to Bonds Street with their cloth ripped and messed up hair......

There were a lot of situations where I had to help my sister. I was always there.... Things were no different as adults....

In the following you will see how close we were that was scary....

I used to think that my sister was part of a Central plan made by God....

It is easy to say that a person has a serious advantage in life if they come from a loving and supportive family. Many people still succeed even though they come from less-than-ideal family situations.

By having our basic needs and knowing that our parents loved us, it made it better to cope with all the challenges of day-to-day living. It was much easier to face any obstacle as we grew older.

Adelin and I were always coming up with different ideas to help around the house. My mom didn't know how to handle simple everyday problems. She used to tell us to wait for our father to come home. We got tired of that answer; therefore, we made our own decisions without telling her.

This was no coincidence. I truly believe that God organized us into families so that we can grow up in happiness and safety. Sometimes I think that we learned to love each other selflessly. It was the key to true joy.

Our neighbors were not surprised that we graduated from high school with honors and went on to college. My sister, brothers and I had a dream. That dream came true. It was to finish our education and be ready for the future.

Our family always came first. Perhaps we were one of the lucky ones who were raised in a happy and secure household with two loving parents. Likely, as adults, we wanted the same happy environment for our family. Now a day, living peacefully in a family isn't easy. For us, family values were number one. Those values taught by our parents strengthen our family.

Many people who have lived through disasters never say, "All I could think about during the earthquake was my bank account." They always say, "All I could think about was family." It shouldn't require a disaster for us to know that this is the truth.

When we were growing up, we made a pledge. I reminded my siblings that we were a team. No one would even dare to bother us because we were there for each other.

We made believe that were actors in a play. I told them to think of the parts we had or will play in our family role. We looked at all the responsibilities that went along with each one of us. We all put a lot of effort in strengthening our family.

I am saying this because we moved to New York and my parents weren't ready to raise us there. Things were very complicated in the new environment. In Puerto Rico, my parents had it all.

We were always helping our parents by keeping a peaceful home. We never complain about anything. My sister and two brothers helped me by putting each other's needs first. We never bother to ask for new clothes or toys. All four of us learned how to recycle at a very young age. We never got discouraged.

No matter how hard things were, we tried to keep our home almost perfect...

I remember one Christmas day that we told our parents that we were happy by just getting hats and gloves as gifts. I promised my sister and brothers that I would save every penny to buy what we really wanted without letting our parents know.

Guess what? We did fine. Since we were so good in school, we all put together a business. I told Papa John that we needed a typewriter to do our schoolwork. I started typing term papers. My brother Papo did the covers. Julio did some writing and my sister put all the papers together. We made a couple of dollars weekly. We had so much money that we bought leather coats and nice outfits.

Sometimes Papa John would borrow from us. He had to pay back with interest of course.

As we got older, the boys drifted apart, but my sister and I remained close....

When I got married, my sister was the one that gave me the money needed for the reception. We both paid for the whole event. We even bought my mother's dress, shoes, and accessories. We paid for the rental of my father's tux.

A couple of years later, my sister was getting married. Once again, we both paid for everything. We never bother our parents with our problems of monetary expenses. My dad just paid the necessary bills for the house.

If my mom needed anything, my sister and I were there to buy it. My mother never asked for much. We spoiled her all the time. My father was happy because he didn't spend anything on my mother.

Even after we got married, we took care of our parents. They moved to Puerto Rico, and we mailed them packages and money....

Chapter 2

My Nephews

Ray and Rebustino

A person can learn a lot from books, but many things can only be learned the hard way. What do I mean by this? Well, one can learn by living, suffering, or even enjoying life. I am sitting here thinking about my family. There were many lessons learned. We were so close, and we always took care of each other.

One evening, at approximately 7 p.m., I was in my room in Ponce. The weather was pleasant; however, it was too quiet. Suddenly, my dogs began to bark. I got worried. I thought that maybe they saw someone trying to break in.

If they kept barking, I would have to go downstairs. I was trying to get up from my bed, but I went down. I thought of the many lessons I've learned in life would end up at the bottom of rubbish or something. I could only tell you that everything in the room started shaking. I couldn't move at all.

A heavy-duty magnetic field was pulling me toward the ground. This weird sensation lasted a couple of minutes. I thought that it was the end of the world. I turned the T.V. on and to my surprise, there was a newsflash of an earthquake that just hit Puerto Rico.

I went to check on my dogs and they were still shivering. They came into the house, and I calmed them down. I let them stay on the sofa until morning. I then decided to write what had happened so that my nephews could read it after I am gone. I hope they'll find it useful.

I'm writing this today, April 24, 2016, so that you, Ray and Rebustino, can get an idea that life is too short to waste. There are many reasons that I started writing about the earth shocking event. I feared the earthquake might really destroy me.

All the lessons I've learned in life would have disappeared with me. By writing this, I hope to pass on a few of my memories to you and the rest of my family.

The most important message that I want to bring across is that most things you worry about will not bother you the next day. A year later you will not even be able to remember them if you try.

As you get older, you will not worry about what grades you got in high school or college. You are not even worrying about the games you lost when you were in the little leagues. You won't worry about what other people think about you.

Most of the things you worry about now will never happen. Life will still go on no matter what. Please learn to enjoy every day and try to enjoy it as if it is your last. It has taken me a long time to understand this, and I wish I had understood it sooner.

Happiness is not a destination but a journey. You will never be smart enough, or rich enough. Whatever it is you want, there is always something better. Enjoy the journey of learning, working, and living. If you enjoy the journey, you'll probably achieve a lot more than if you focused on goals.

If you do decide you want to be "successful", I can give you the formula for success. There are only three things you need to do:

First, decide exactly what it is you want.

Second, determine the price you will have to pay.

Third, and this is the hardest and most important part, pay the price.

Material things don't make you happy, but memories will always stay with you. Whatever it is that you buy, you will soon get used to it. It will make you happy for a short while, but it will not make you happy forever.

I can't even remember most of the toys I've had in my life, but I still think of my times with your mother, my brothers, and your grandparents. Life then was full of happiness.

I remember walking with your mother to school and how happy we were. I also remember hugging your grandma when I came home from school. Those memories will never go away.

Your family is the most important thing you have in life. Friends, boyfriends, girlfriends, and co-workers come and go, but the only thing that you can always count on is your family. If you find a friend who is always there for you, you're extremely lucky. They exist, but they're very rare.

Rebustino, one day, you will have your own family. Ray, you have yours. You guys must love them and look after them. You will understand in the future that just as your grandmother and father died, your mother will die as well. Strive to be good sons.

Don't be surprised if one day you will be like your parents. Your parents were not perfect, and you will not be either, but you can be loving and good.

Never stop learning, and always be ready to teach yourself things you don't know. The only things you will remember are things you care about. No one can teach you everything you need to know. You will also forget most of what you study, and that is fine.

Remember to always stay curious, and you'll be surprised how much you can learn. Let me tell you something that when people speak of intelligence, what they generally mean is curiosity.

All great discoveries start with a question. Children are born curious, and school can beat it out of you. Never stop asking questions.

Ray and Rebustino, you're never too old to learn. I want you two to promise me that you are never going to live someone else's life. Find your gifts and the things that give you pleasure, develop those gifts, and pursue them. Do what makes you happy and be great at it. You have skills and gifts that no one will ever have or see again.

I think that's very important when you learn how to cope in life. Once you learn how, you'll want to change it and make it better. It is up to you to decide whether you will be strong or not. Many people suffer great tragedies and live full and happy lives.

Remember the people you love. Accept those terrible things that may happen. Try to live as if each day is your last with those you love. There is nothing else you can do.

Currently, I want to thank you both for letting me be part of your lives. You both gave me a chance to be not only your aunt, but also your second mother. Sometimes I laugh at the things we did together. I always looked forward to each of your birthdays, little leagues games, school plays, graduations and much more.

I remember very clearly those summer days in Massapequa. We used to be at the pool very early. You guys were taking swimming lessons. I was very impressed when within days you both learned how to swim.

I was always present at every birthday party. Your mother and I would pick up a theme to decorate the basement or park. As always, I was the clown. I believe I had more fun than the kids....

There were other funny occasions that I remember clearly. Rebustino and I went to see lots of movies. After each show, we would go to a restaurant. Rebustino was a perfect gentleman. While eating, we would chat about the movie.

We went to see Titanic, The Mask, and The Flintstone just to name a few. I really enjoyed every moment spent with you two.

Sometimes your parents would go out and I stayed babysitting. We played with your Nintendo, electronic bowling machine and even yatzee.

I hope you still remember those happy times because I will never forget them.

Today, I am very sad. My dear sister, Adelin, is not here anymore. She loved you guys so much. I never saw a caring mother loving her kids so much. I wanted her to live with me in Puerto Rico. She told me no because she still has you two. I was furious because she was always alone during every holiday....

In the following you will read about my father and grandfather. They were in the Puerto Rico National Guard. Things were rough for everyone in the states and Puerto Rico during that time...

Chapter 3

Father and Son fighting
for the Same Cause

In the early spring, in 1950, The National Guard Army was training every soldier harder than ever. Everyone knew that soon the National Guard would be mobilized.

My mother and grandmother were sad during those days because they knew that every member in my family would be deployed to Korea.

Since my mother was pregnant with her second child, she was too big to work around the house. My grandmother, Guadalupe, let her rest because my mother was due soon. This time, both my grandmother Guadalupe and my great-grandmother had a bad feeling about this child.

My mother was always too tired and didn't want to eat. I guess my mom was always sick because she didn't see my father often enough.

On October 20, 1950, my mother went into labor for more hours than expected. She gave birth to another baby girl, my sister Adelin. My grandmother Lupe and great grandma Dolores were happy because the baby was small, but healthy.

My mother wanted to know if my father was around. My father and grandfather were doing drill at Lucille Field base known today as Fort Allen in Juana Diaz, Puerto Rico. Both my father and grandfather were happy because the new baby was doing well. They both wanted to go home, but all passes were denied.

My father got very angry. He just wanted an hour pass to see his wife and daughters. The answer from the commander was no....

My father decided to jump the fence...

So, when his unit went on break, he started walking very fast. There were sugar cane fields and farms before reaching the main road. As soon as he reached the street, a car stopped and to my father's surprise, it was his commander. The commander looked at him and told him to get in the car. My father was surprised because he was escorted to Ponce to see the family.

The commander told him to stay the rest of the evening, but to return to the base the following day. My mother was very happy to see him. Adelin and I were beside my mom when my dad arrived. The whole family had a wonderful night together.

During the months that followed, things were very rough. Lots of soldiers were sent to Korea. My grandfather and my father were waiting for their orders...

Our nation was facing one of the worst times of that era. Puerto Rico was waiting and willing to fight in Korea. I am proud to say, that my father, CSM Juan José Pagán Rodriguez, of the Puerto Rico National Guard and my grandfather, Staff Sergeant Julio Pagán Torres, now deceased, were among those brave soldiers fighting for our country in one of the bloodiest conflicts.

To understand the commotion that was going on in the states and Puerto Rico, I will give you some facts of what our soldiers were facing during that time....

On July 1, 1950, the Army's 24th Infantry Division became the first U.S. troop to arrive in Korea. They were transferred from Japan passing through the Port of Pusan. The troops took up Positions in Taejon, about 75 miles south of Seoul.

A couple of days later on July 19, 1950, the 25th Infantry arrived followed by the 1st Marine Brigade and the 2nd Infantry Division in late July.

Things were getting worse in Korea that on July 20, 1950, the casualties were increasing. More than 2,400 men or 30% were reported dead. Taejon fell under the arms of the enemy.

All Americans and the rest of world were alarmed. This meant that many were going to be called to serve their country. The Reserves and the National Guard will be mobilized.

Puerto Rico, a beautiful island located in the Caribbean, and a Commonwealth of the United States, was getting ready. There was no cultural or language barrier holding those brave men. Those "Boricuas" were well trained. Three members of my family were in the National Army Guard.

They knew that it wouldn't be long for the guard to be call for active duty. All three were ready to serve their nation. They were Staff Sgt. Julio Pagan Torres, my grandfather, assigned to 65th Infantry 4 machine gun 30 calibers, Sgt. Juan J. Pagan Rodriguez, my father, assigned to 65th Infantry Heavy Mortal Co. and the youngest, my uncle, Cpl. Julio Pagan Rodríguez was assigned to Artillery.

By early September, the new troops were combat ready in hardened fighting units. The Puerto Rican National Guard was mobilized on September 10, 1950. Every "Boricua's" family was worried because their loved ones will leave to an unknown land. Many have never been abroad. Now, they must face a lot of hardships.

It didn't take long for a humble family in Ponce to hear the worst news ever. Their sons and husbands must report for duty. This was awful because all three soldiers were assigned to infantry or artillery.

The women were devastated when they heard the news on the radio. Staff Sgt. Julio Pagan Torres and Sgt. Juan J. Pagan Rodriguez received their orders. Their unit, the 65th Infantry was being mobilized. Cpl. Julio Pagan Rodriguez wasn't called at this time.

The 65th Infantry was now divided. That meant father and son were separated. The 296 Infantry was sent to Tortuguero. They were divided into two groups, 2nd to Juana Diaz and the 3rd to Cayey.

Chapter 4

Waiting for the Worst

Everything was moving too fast. The Puerto Rico National Guard was giving orders left and right. There was no question asked. It didn't matter if there was one sole survivor in a family.

Men were needed to go abroad and fight for their country. Sgt. Juan J. Pagán Rodriguez was ready to fight; however, he had a young wife and two young children. Sgt. Julio Pagán Torres also had young ones. They had a big problem.

There was also a possibility that Cpl. Julio Pagán Rodriguez might be called to active duty. They wanted to serve, but they had a family.

The following day, both father and son decided to speak to their commander. The commander found it quite unusual for members of the same family to be called to active duty.

He listened to their petition and wrote all the information given by my father and grandfather. He told Sgt. Juan Pagán Rodriguez that he was the one chosen to go to Korea and that Sgt. Julio Pagán Torres will stay in Puerto Ri-co.

What follows will not only put you in tears but will make you wonder.

In November 1950, Sgt. Juan J. Pagán Rodriguez said goodbye to his beloved wife and family. He was only 22 years old but was fully aware of his commitment. His father promised him that he would take care of the whole family. Sgt. Juan J. Pagán Rodriguez just said, "Bendición Papito" and got on the bus…

Many "Boricuas" were also leaving Puerto Rico. This was the saddest day for the whole island. Saying goodbye was very hard. The 65th Infantry had already sent soldiers to Korea. Those first infantry soldiers made history throughout the nation. They were known as "The Borinqueneers" The 65th Infantry Regiment started the assault on January 31, 1951.

NO WORD FROM SGT JUAN PAGAN RODRIGUEZ

The Pagán family was very confused during this crisis because right after Sgt. Juan J. Pagán Rodriguez left Puerto Rico, his father Staff Sgt. Julio Pagán received new orders.

These orders stated that he was leaving for Korea in December 1950. This was the worst Christmas gift that anyone could receive. Now Staff Sgt. Julio Pagán Torres was also leaving his family. He told his wife, Guadalupe, "No te apures, todo va a salir bien".

He couldn't face his daughter-in-law, Digna. She was holding her youngest daughter Adelin. Digna was too upset to say goodbye. Sgt. Juan J. Pagán Rodriguez left the island months before and no one knew his whereabouts.

The so many visits to the Red Cross were made in vain. Sgt. Julio Pagán Torres even went to his commander for an answer of his previous visit. The commander apologized for the awful mess and stated that he was sorry. Sgt. Pagán Torres asked about the previous order.

The commander could only say that they were revoked because they got to Washing-ton too late. Communication was very slow in those days…….

ILL FEELINGS IN THE FRONT LINES

Sgt. Juan J. Pagán Rodriguez was already fighting in the front lines. He got to Korea in January 1951 and at this point he was uneasy. He had been away from his family for nearly two months and no news was received.

It was hard to get anything where he was stationed. His new acquired family was his buddies, fellow "BORICUAS". All of them were waiting for some kind of news from Puerto Rico.

In Ponce, Puerto Rico, things weren't that great. With the breadwinner gone, it wasn't easy to raise all those children. Guadalupe and Digna had to go to the Red Cross. They wanted to hear news from their husbands.

The Red Cross assured them that both father and son were fine. Food and emergency money were provided. Digna was worried because the youngest daughter was very ill. Adelin was a very fragile child and needed medical attention.

When the Red Cross saw the baby, they referred her to the best doctors. The child was well taken care of and recovered within months.

By the end of February, troops were sent to the front lines once again....

IN KOREA

One morning, Sgt. Juan Jose Pagán Rodriguez was ordered to take a couple of guys to a designated area. Sgt. Pagán Rodriguez briefed his men and started walking. It was a cold bitter day and there was a lot of snow on the ground. The young soldiers were still trying to get used to that weather.

They were all melancholy because they missed their sunny and warm Puerto Rico. Many had suffered from frost bites. It wasn't easy keeping those soldiers motivated. They haven't heard anything from their families in months.

As they were walking, Sgt. Pagán Rodriguez started telling funny stories. The soldiers felt at ease. They reached their destination point. There were many wounded and others were suffering from the cold. Sgt. Pagán Rodriguez and his Troop relieved those men.

The fire never stopped. Sgt. Pagán Rodriguez has been in his post for nearly a week. He was hungry and so were his men. They needed clean uniforms and chow.

Sgt. Juan J. Pagán Rodriguez kept fighting even though he didn't receive any news from Puerto Rico.

Suddenly, he received a message. He was ordered to report to his Commander. The young sergeant was surprised, but at the same time was happy to take a shower and change his uniform. He was escorted to his superior and to his surprise there was Staff Sergeant Julio Pagán Torres waiting for him.

Words couldn't describe the emotion that those two human beings were feeling. Tears of joy were rolling down their faces. Sgt. Pagán Rodriguez asked his father about the family. He was also puzzled and questioning his father's arrival…both….in Korea…

The Commander of the 65th Infantry told both father and son that they would have to wait for new orders. He also told them that they will leave for Puerto Rico soon….

Those orders never came. Sgt. Juan J. Pagán Rodriguez was once again separated from his father……

A couple of days have gone by….

Sgt. Juan J. Pagán Rodriguez and his men were going to another camp site. They had a couple of jeeps with plenty of supplies.

Sgt. Pagán Rodriguez saw a troop right in front of him. They were going to the same unit.

At that point, Sgt. Juan Pagán Rodriguez got the surprise of his life. His father, Staff Sgt. Julio Pagán Torres was among those men! He called his father, and both rode on the same jeep.

Once they arrived at their designated area, their new commandant called them. This time he gave them written orders. That was the best news Sgt. Pagán Rodriguez had received. He was going home, and his father was going with him safe and sound.

Sgt. Pagán Rodriguez and Staff Sgt. Julio Pagán Torres didn't want to be part of the big reception that was waiting for them in Puerto Rico.....

They were the first father and son wearing the same uniform and fighting for the same cause, but they just wanted to see their family.

They went to Ponce without being noticed. The taxi driver was the only witness when they reached home. There were a few gathered in front of the house. None of them were aware that a taxi had stopped there.

The two sergeants got out of the taxi very quietly and opened the gate. Digna and Guadalupe started running once they saw them. It was a great day for the Pagán Family.

Staff Sergeant Julio Pagán Torres and Sergeant Juan J. Pagán Rodríguez were the first father and son to serve the nation. They were in combat together and together returned home to Puerto Rico.

The Korean War brought Puerto Rican soldiers their greatest visibility, highest awards, and most punishing losses. There were 43, 434 Puerto Ricans in this war and 39, 591 of them were volunteers.

The 65th Infantry was chosen to guard the nation. They received awards for their bravery. It was also the last group of soldiers to leave the combat zone...

Some bullets were whizzing by them as they boarded the ship to evacuate.......

For that a great SALUTE TO OUR "BORICUA" Korean's Heroes. We will never forget them. CSM Juan J. Pagán Rodriguez was very proud of being a soldier during the Korean Conflict...

Chapter 5

Dolores Rodriguez Quiles
1884-1972

Once again, I must write about my great grandmother and the rest of our relatives. I am doing this to show you that were a very loving and caring family....

Dolores Rodriguez Quiles was born in 1884 and died in 1972. Who was this lady? Well, she was my great grandmother. She was born in Adjuntas, Puerto Rico. Her father was a Spaniard merchant, Vicente Rodriguez, and her mother a high society Spaniard, Lucia Quiles.

Let me take you back in time so that you may get an idea how two young Spaniard met in Puerto Rico and started a family. Spanish immigration to Puerto Rico began in 1493 and it continued until 1898. Puerto Rico at that time was a colony of Spain.

On September 25, 1493, Christopher Columbus set sail on his second voyage with 17 ships and 1,200–1,500 men from Cádiz, Spain.

On November 19, 1493, he landed on the island, naming it San Juan Bautista in honor of Saint John the Baptist.

The first Spanish settlement, Caparra, was founded on 8 August 1508 by Juan Ponce de León, born in Valladolid, Spain, a lieutenant under Columbus, who later became the first governor of Puerto Rico.

The following year the settlement was abandoned in favor of a nearby island on the coast, named Puerto Rico, Rich Port, which had a suitable harbor.

In 1511, a second settlement, San German, was established in the southwestern part of the island.

During the 1520s the island took the name of Puerto Rico while the port became San Juan. The Spanish heritage in Puerto Rico is profound today in its customs and many traditions, language, and in the old and new architectural designs.

The European heritage of Puerto Ricans comes primarily from one source: Spaniards including, Canarians, Asturians, Catalans, Galicians, Castilians, Andalusians, and Basques.

From the beginning of the conquest of Puerto Rico, Castilians ruled over the religious Roman Catholicism and political life. Some came to the island for just a few years and then returned to Spain, however, many stayed.

Among Puerto Rico's founding families were the Castilian Ponce de León family. Their home was built in 1521 by Ponce de Leon but he died in the same year, leaving "La Casa Blanca", or "The White House", to his young son Luis Ponce de León.

The original structure didn't last long; two years after its construction a hurricane destroyed it, and it was rebuilt by Ponce de León's son-in-law Juan García Troche.

The descendants of Ponce de León's family lived in La Casa Blanca for more than 250 years when in 1779 the Spanish Army took control of it. Finally, the American military moved into La Casa Blanca in 1898.

The southern city of Ponce is named after Juan Ponce de León y Loayza, the great-grandson of the island's first governor. Immigration to the island caused the population to grow rapidly during the 19th century.

In 1800, the population was 155,426 and ended the century with almost one million inhabitants, 953,243, multiplying the population by about six times.

The major motivation for the massive European immigration during the 1800s was the Spanish Crown's proclamation of the Royal Decree of Graces of 1815, Real Cédula de Gracias, which led to the arrival of primarily Catholic immigrants from some seventy-four countries.

Puerto Rico, during the 19th century, was very well known to every European country. Among them were hundreds of Corsicans, French, Irish, German, Scottish, Italian, Lebanese, Maltese, Dutch, and English and Portuguese families moving to the island.

Some countries were represented by only a few immigrants, i.e., fifty-one Chinese immigrants during this century. The country that still sent the most people was Spain.

From the start of colonization, other groups from Andalusia, Catalonia, Asturias, Galicia, and Majorca had also immigrated, although the Canarian people formed the basis.

Guess what? Once the 19th century came, things changed drastically. According to Puerto Rican authors such as Estela Cifre de Loubriel, who did extensive research on immigration patterns to the island, during the 19th century the greatest number of Spaniards that came to the island with large families were Catalans and Mallorcans.

It is important to know about immigration during that time so that you can visualize what was going on on the island during the 18th and 19th century. My great grandparents, like many Spaniards, met during family reunions.

Since both great grandparents came from a well to do family, it was easy to meet in extraordinary events of high society of that era.

My great great-grandfather, Vicente Rodriguez, was 17 yrs. old when he met my great great-grandmother Lucia Quiles.

Lucia was also 17 yrs. old. Both families were incredibly happy when the two love birds announced that they wanted to get married. They knew from the beginning that Vicente and Lucia were a blessed couple.

In June 1883, Vicente and Lucia got married in the Guadalupe Catholic Cathedral of Ponce. Vicente and Lucia were happy in Adjuntas,

Puerto Rico. They received a piece of land full of crops and a huge house with housekeepers. All came from both the Rodriquez and Quiles families.

In Ponce, they received stores and a couple of clients from Spain.

After a couple of days after their honeymoon, the newlyweds went to visit their parents. The families, the Quiles and the Rodriguez, were happy to see the young couple. They wanted to tell them something very important. The Vicente and Lucia got very anxious. They were surprised to hear that both families wanted to talk to them.

Vicente Rodriguez Sr. told his son that he was returning to Spain. He was going to leave his business in Puerto Rico because in Madrid he had other properties that needed to be taken care of.

Lucia's parents had a similar situation. They also had properties in Spain and wanted to go for a visit. They told the newlyweds that they were ready to leave because their son, Vicente Jr., and Lucia, can now run their fortunes in Puerto Rico.

Vicente and Lucia said their goodbyes to both the Quiles and Rodriguez families. They were sad because Spain was very far. A trip to Europe took over a month.

During the year that followed, Vicente and Lucia were again blessed. They welcomed their gorgeous child, Dolores Rodriguez Quiles, to their loving family.

Dolores' upbringing was superb. Since living in Puerto Rico, she acquired a lot of knowledge from the diverse cultures on the island.

Also, she was fascinated because she got the chance of meeting some Taínos Indians.

Vicente and Lucia decided to relocate to Ponce. It was a great town for merchants. In addition, they kept their coffee and tobacco fields in Adjuntas.

In the town of Ponce, they had their stores and clients. Dolores was doing well in her studies. She had a good head for business.

Dolores has grown up by now. Her parents were now thinking of her future. She had lots of friends both males and females. She told her parents that she was not rushing into any marriage at this time.

Vicente and Lucia had other worries. Their parents were in Spain, and it was not easy staying connected with them. Many merchants told them that their parents' business in Europe had doubled; however, it was getting hard to communicate with Puerto Rico.

Puerto Rico was growing fast not only in its culture, but also it was becoming a mine for commerce. The politicians were getting scared because at beginning all rules came from Spain. Well to do families knew that they could be elected governors of the island if they wished.

Now....it was getting harder...

Dolores was having fun because her friends were mostly artists, authors, song writers and musicians. She knew that someday she would get marry, but not now.... Life for her was great....

Dolores parents weren't getting any younger. She was their only offspring. They wanted grandchildren. Both Vicente and Lucia wanted to go to Spain, but they didn't want to leave their daughter.

Dolores told them time after time that she was happy leading the life she was leading. She was aware of her fortune and so were the guys she met. She didn't want to end up supporting any male.

Dolores Rodriguez Quiles, my great grandma, knew Puerto Rico was going through hard times. She kept up with the latest news because her friends told her about the United States and Europe. Things in the island were not the same. Every day something was happening.

The trading with Europe was getting slower. The politicians were facing big threads from the United States.

Finally, it did happen...... the Spanish American War 0f 1898.

During the Spanish-American War, United States forces launch their invasion in Puerto Rico, the 108-mile-long, 40-mile-wide Island that as one of Spain's two principal possessions in the Caribbean was now under fire. With little resistance and only seven deaths, U.S. troops under General Nelson A. Miles were able to secure the island by mid-August.

After the signing of an armistice with Spain, American troops raised the U.S. flag over the island, formalizing U.S. authority over its one million inhabitants.

In December, of the same year, the Treaty of Paris was signed, ending the Spanish-American War, and officially approving the cession of Puerto Rico to the United States. The Spaniard, living on the island, suffered a lot during the war. The well to do merchants, store owners and high society were getting ready to leave Puerto Rico.

The United States informed them that everything they owned will be taken away if they didn't leave.

So, the rich left the island.......

When Dolores' family was ready to relocate to Spain, the hurricane season was about to start....

On August 8, 1899, Puerto Rico experienced one of the most destructive hurricanes in history. It rained for 28 days straight, and the winds reached speeds of 100 miles per hour. This was Hurricane San Ciriaco.

The most devastating effect of San Ciriaco was the destruction of the farmlands, especially in the mountains where the coffee plantations were located. San Ciriaco aggravated the social and economic situation of Puerto Rico at the time and had serious repercussions in the years that followed.

The losses of life and property damage were immense. Approximately 3,400 people died in the floods and thousands were left without shelter, food, or work. Dolores' parents died during the hurricane.

They were hit by the heavy storms and their house was washed away. Nothing happened to Dolores because she was in San Juan visiting some friends....

After Dolores' loss, she had no place to go. The coffee fields and tobacco fields were destroyed. She tried extremely hard to locate her grandparents in Spain. They never responded to her many messages. Some merchants told her that it was hard getting information from Spain because the Americans were keeping an eye on them.

Dolores had money in the bank; however, with the change from Spaniard to American money she was left with no money whatsoever.

Dolores never gave up. She started going to the seaport trying to get some source of news from Spain.

She failed... The Americans were all over....

During those visits to the seaport, which is when she met a young merchant by the name of Amparo Manfredi. This man was very handsome. Dolores hesitated in dating. He kept insisting until she accepted him as her boyfriend.

Dolores was very jealous because Amaparo had lots of friends. He was only six months in Puerto Rico and the other six at sea. She didn't really know this man. He did not promise her marriage either. Amparo only told her that he was in love with her. It was hard to trust someone like him.

On one of his visits to Puerto Rico in 1904, Dolores told Amparo that she was pregnant. He just looked at her. He stayed long enough to give the baby his name.

Amparo Manfredi Jr. was born on June 10, 1904. He was a healthy child. Dolores was happy to become a mother, but had mixed feelings because Amparo Manfredi Sr. He disappeared from her life.

Once again, Dolores Rodriguez Quiles had to start a new life, and this time with a child. Slowly Dolores forgot about being Spaniard or anything that had to do with Spain. She started thinking about her future.

"Bomba y plena" was on her mind...

Dancing was always on her mind even though she could work in any business environment. She wasn't satisfied...

One afternoon, she was looking out her office's window. She saw a couple of wagons. Those wagons had all sorts of signs advertising that they were a traveling theater. They showed up at the port because many ships stopped in Puerto Rico to leave merchandise from different countries.

Dolores was very curious when she saw the dancers. She thought that it was easier to dance than to sit in an office all day long.

She ran down the stairs. Once, outside, she met with the director of the group. She told him that she was a dancer. He greeted her and informed her that an audition was going to be held in the afternoon.

As she was getting ready to dance, Jose Mercusi was also getting ready to perform. Jose was the lead dancer of the traveling theater. This theater was made up of dancers and actors from Spain and some locals.

Spaniard valet dancers joined the "mestizo" in the island. This was a big turn out because when Spaniard and the mestizo worked together the music, songs, dancers, and rhythm changed for the best.

This is where the Caribbean tone came about. Dancing was a complete turnaround, and I am proud to say that my great-grandmother, Dolores Rodriguez Quiles, was part of that change.

Traditional, folk, and popular music did change when the Spaniard mixed with the African.

Some facts about the early music in Puerto Rico:

Music culture in Puerto Rico during the 16th, 17th, and 18th centuries is poorly documented. Certainly, it included Spanish church music, military band music, and diverse genres of dance music cultivated by the "jíbaros". The "Jibaros" were the peasants of Puerto Rico.

The "jibaros" or peasants never constituted more than 11% of the is-land's population, however, they contributed some of the island's most dynamic musical features becoming distinct indeed.

In the 19th century, Puerto Rican music begins to emerge into historical daylight, with notated genres like the "danza". The "danza" was recognized as better than the folk genres.

At that time, the "jíbaro" music and "bomba y plena" weren't really documented or recognized as music. I guess it was because of its origin. The "danza" came from the Spaniard and the jibaro music and "bomba y plena" from the mestizo....

The African people of Puerto Rico used drums made of carved solid wood covered with an untreated rawhide on one side, commonly made from goatskin. A popular word derived from creole to design this drum was "shukbwa", which literally means 'trunk of tree'.

In other islands like Guadalupe, this type of hollowed trunk is called "bwa fuyé".

The classical valet dancers' steps also changed with time....

Jíbaro music

"Jibaros" are small farmers of primarily Hispanic descent. They constituted most of the Puerto Rican population until the mid-twentieth century.

They are traditionally recognized as romantic icons of land cultivation, hard work and self-sufficiency, hospitality, and love of song and dance.

Their instruments were relatives of the Spanish "vihuela", especially the "cuatro" which evolved from four single strings to five pairs. There is also the lesser known "tiple".

A typical jíbaro group nowadays might feature a "cuatro", guitar, and percussion instrument such as the "guiro" scraper and/or bongo.

Lyrics to "jíbaro" music are generally in the "décima" form, consisting of ten octosyllabic lines in the rhyme scheme abba, accddc. "Décima" form derives from 16th-century Spain. Although it has largely died out in that country except the Canaries, it took root in various places in Latin America especially Cuba and Puerto Rico where it is sung in diverse styles.

A sung "decima" might be pre-composed, derived from a publication by some literati, or ideally, improvised on the spot, especially in the of a "controversia" in which two singer-poets trade witty insults or argue on some topic. In between the "décimas", lively improvisations can be played on the "cuatro". This music form is also known as "Tipica" as well as "Tropical".

The décimas are sung to stock melodies, with standardized cuatro accompaniment patterns. About twenty such song-types are in common use.

Explanation of the structure of the "decima".

They are grouped into two broad categories, viz., seis e.g., seis fajardeño, seis chorreao and Aguinaldo.

Aguinaldo:

There are diverse types of aguildando:
The "Aguinaldo Orocoveño" from the Town of Orocovis
The "Aguinaldo Cayeyano" from the town of Cayes
Traditionally, the seis could accompany dancing, but this tradition has largely died out except in tourist shows and festivals.

Let me explain the "Aguinaldo."

The "Aguinaldo" is most characteristically sung during the Christmas season, when groups of revelers "parrandas" go from house to house, singing jíbaro songs and partying. The "Aguinaldo" texts are not about Christmas, and unlike Anglo-American Christmas carols, they are sung by a solo with the other revelers singing chorus.

In general, the Christmas season is a time when traditional music, both seis and Aguinaldo, is most likely to be heard.

Fortunately, many groups of Puerto Ricans are dedicated to preserving traditional music by continued practice. Jíbaro music came to be marketed on commercial recordings in the twentieth century, and singer poets like Ramito, Flor Morales Ramos, born 1915 and died in 1990.

All these types of music are well documented, however, jíbaros themselves were becoming an endangered species, as agribusiness and urbanization have drastically reduced the numbers of small farmers in the island.

Many "jíbaro" songs dealt accordingly with the changes of migration to New York.

"Jíbaro" music has in general declined accordingly, although it retains its place in local culture, especially around Christmas time, and special social gatherings.

There are many cuatro players, some of whom have cultivated exceptional and unique techniques.

Both of my great grandparents were aware of the change in dancing and melodies throughout the whole island. Music brought them together. They both knew how to compose, sing decimas and how to dance the "the danza" and "bomba y plena".

Years went by and Jose and Dolores were getting older.... They started working elsewhere....

Jose Mercusi was working as a security guard at the "Matilde" sugar cane fields. He worked night shifts, and it was impossible to get a good rest. He was always in a bad mood.

Dolores, in the other hand, kept her other ambition alive. She kept working in hospitals nearby. She acquired a lot of knowledge and graduated as a midwife.

Jose had other things in mind....

One Sunday morning he told Dolores to iron his best clothing. It was a white jacket and white pants. She cleaned and ironed the suit....

You are not going to believe what happened next.

By midafternoon, the rumors around the neighborhood were saying that Jose was getting married with Lorenza Sabater...

Dolores was terribly angry because she was really in loved with this man. They had one daughter, Guadalupe, who he never admitted was his. He never gave her his last name....

By now, Dolores had two children. The oldest child was Amparo Manfredi Jr. and the youngest Guadalupe Rodriguez.

She was taking classes in "Hospital Damas". This hospital was founded in 1863 as "Santo Asilo de Damas" by Sister Francisca Paz Cabrera. It was attended to by the group known as "Siervas de Maria", Servants of Mary, since 1891.

The hospital was in downtown Ponce, but on 6 May 1973, it moved to its current location at a new 10-story tower on the north side of the Ponce By-Pass.

The original location of Damas, as the current hospital is commonly called, is now home to Parque Urbano Dora Colón Clavell.

Dolores was always eager to learn more. She was learning from the best nurses in the hospital. She also got involved in delivering babies. That is how she began to study for her licenses as a "partera."

Dolores Rodriguez Quiles graduated as a midwife, "partera". She assisted nurses and doctors in the hospital to be certified.

Dolores Rodriguez Quiles never met Mr. Right....

Her last sole mate was Chito Lugo. They had two children Ramon Lugo and Constancia. Guess what? He did not give Costancia Rodriguez his last name....

Today, after we all watched her blow out the ridiculous number of candles on her 100th birthday cake, my great grandmother looked up at all of us. She was happy to see her children, grandchildren, great grandchildren, and extended family and said, "Look what I started this lovely family. I am so proud to be a part of your lives."

She started telling us her stories....

Mamá Dolores told us how she did her dancing and singing at "Juan Francisco Sabater Night Club". She worked there only on weekends because she took care of the sick during the week.

Sometimes I say that she was born before her time. Mamá Dolores had the skills of becoming a great physician. She also used to assist a doctor that came to the community once a month.

While waiting for the doctor one afternoon, she decided to write on her journal which was required by law during that time.

One day, she was writing a cure for stomach ulcers. She wrote down how "yerva mora", a plant grown all over Puerto Rico, may cure any stomach virus.

There was a man that was complaining for over a week about the pain. He told him to make tea out of the green plant and to add honey and milk.

When the doctor came to visit him, the pain was gone. The doctor informed him to go to the hospital for some analysis. He did and was diagnosed free of stomach virus or ulcer.

Mamá Dolores was an angel. She didn't charge anyone for her services. She just wished them well. There are so many stories about this wonderful lady.

Mamá Dolores saw Puerto Rico during the Spaniard era and during the invasion of the Americans. She saw many changes on this beautiful island.

During the first three decades of its rule, the U.S. government made efforts to Americanize its new possession, including granting full U.S. citizenship to Puerto Ricans in 1917 and considering a measure that would make English the island's official language.

Also, during the 1930s, a nationalist movement led by the Popular Democratic Party won wide support across the island, and further U.S. assimilation was successfully opposed.

Beginning in 1948, Puerto Ricans could elect their own governor, and in 1952 the U.S. Congress approved a new Puerto Rican constitution that made the island an autonomous U.S. commonwealth, with its citizens retaining American citizenship.

The constitution was formally adopted by Puerto Rico on July 25, 1952, the 54th anniversary of the U.S. invasion.

The movements for Puerto Rican statehood, along with lesser movements for Puerto Rican independence, have won supporters on the island. However, the popular referendums in 1967 and 1993 demonstrated that the majority of Puerto Ricans still supported their special status as a U.S. commonwealth.

Mamá Dolores used to tell me how different it was during the Spaniard Ruling in this island. She also told me about our ancestors. It was so sad listening to her. Tears were rolling down her cheeks as she told me how she had it all and lost it because of the changed in government…

I never understood her sadness until now My dear "Mamá Dolores" my dear great grandmother, I will never forget you………

Chapter 6

Memories of my Grandparents

JULIO PAGAN TORRES
10/10/1902-10/10/1964

I wish you were here, but sad to say that you are gone. I still think of your jokes, laughter, and your adorable smile. I can remember when you and I used to ride for miles.

When I was six, you would drive me to school. I thought to myself, "Gosh, riding with "Abuelo", isn't this cool?"

Sometimes we would stop at the candy store where I would get my "piloncitos", but I always wanted you, Papá Julio, to drive a little more so that my friends would see you in your Army uniform…

Papá Julio, I am now grown up and I wish you could see how smart and bright I became. You lit up my world and put a lot of love in my heart. You helped me with my studies. You and I know that we are not very far apart. I know that you are my guardian angel that watches over me.

There is no one else in the world I would rather it be…

I still miss you and wish you were here. I only must think of you and shed a big tear.

God had to take you home so you would not suffer any more… You were very sick…

Now you are in heaven, and we can't sit on the porch and chat.
I remember all the Army stories and more…
You still live in my heart…
Someday we shall meet again...

GUADALUPE RODRIGUEZ DE PAGAN
February 12, 1909 -May 13, 1997

"My Abuelita"
Dedicated to my dear grandmother.
Guadalupe
If "abuelita" had a meaning
I will tell you what it would be
If you were close to yours
As mine was close to me

"Abuelitas" are always there,
To help you dry your tears.
To pamper and spoil you,
And conquer all your fears.
Even when you did wrong,
And all the wrong you will do.
An "abuelita" will always be there
And unconditionally will always love you.
My "abuelita" inspired me
To follow my every dream
She would tell me that I was not alone
Because we were a team
"Abuelitas" are always busy
And their hearts are very tame
They would tell everyone about you.
Everyone would know your name…
"Abuelitas" will keep everything

From when you're young till now
And when you dance or act on stage,
For her you'll take a bow
Without "abuelitas" we would be lost
And our tears would not be dry.
We will not be encouraged
To spread our wings and fly
To my "abuelita" I want to say Thank You
You will always be in my heart.

MAMA LUPE

What a delight it would be, a heaven with windows…
And guess what? If God granted me a view,
Of all the beauty it beholds, I would only look for you.
I would listen to your laughter that was always.
Music to me, your beautiful long hair and big brown eyes is what I
would wish most to see. If I could only SEE, you one more time.
The smile that warmed my heart,
I would treasure that moment as long as I live, and we
must never depart. Here on earth, I look for you
I pray to God for signs,
Every day that passes by, you are still with me in my mind.
I know you are happy in heaven; you've earned.
your mansion indeed,
I imagine your kitchen table and you waiting there for me.
I love you and I miss you more than words can say…
What I would not give is just to talk to you today.
I hope that you can hear me and listen to my thoughts…
Wherever this life takes me you know
I have not forgotten you.

MY LITTLE SISTER

Remember, that once upon a time I was
blessed and loved by you, it's true,
Mamá Lupe if heaven had at least a window
I would only look for you.

Chapter 7

The Christening

In October 1952, the Pagán Family was celebrating …. My father and grandfather had returned from Korea safely. Also, many of their close friends were among those heroes serving during the Korean Conflict.

My parents decided to have a huge party because all their friends and family are united just like old times.

Since my sister and I were not baptized, they decided to have the Christening the same day. I was already 3 yrs. old and my sister 2 yrs. old.

Even though I was incredibly young, I remember the church ceremony, the party, and the guests. Adelin doesn't remember anything.

What I remember very well about my christening were the outfits my grandmother Mama Lupe made. The dresses were all lace. The shoes were satin and cute tiny socks. Adelin and I looked just like two beautiful princesses from a fairy tale.

<u>At Saint Conrado Church in Ponce Puerto Rico</u> <u>CHRISTENING POEM</u>

There were poems focusing on celebrating the baptism, the admittance of the newly baptized children, Adelin, and Norma into the Christian family. It also conveyed congratulations to the parents and godparents.

There was also a poem said during the rituals ceremony. At the end of the ceremony, there was a Godparent Poem.

This poem deals specifically with the relationship between godparents and godchildren. It also may be a message about the duty of godparents or the honor a godparent feeling for being asked to serve such a role.

All those words were said in Spanish... I heard that story from my mom.

At the party

What I remember about the party was the roasting of a pig. My father hired a couple of guys to do the roasting. My two grandmothers were too busy greeting the guests. My mom was busy with my sister and me.

My cousin, Luis Antonio, oversaw making the ice cream. The good thing about this party was that the whole family participated in putting everything together.

I recall my father chopping big blocks of ice for soda, beer, and juices. As he was getting ready to put the ice in huge iron buckets, he cut his hand. There was blood all over the place. He told my grandfather that it was just a scrape and kept working.

Chapter 8

My Best Friend

I never thought that my sister, Adelin, and I would be as close as we are now. Sure, we still argue with each other, but she is the closest thing to a best friend I will ever have.

You have to say everything started back on October 20, 1950. My mother gave birth to my sister. She was a small baby. My grandmother and great grandmother had a tough time helping my mom deliver.

My father was holding me in another room. I am two years older. When they finally brought me to my mother's room, my sister looked at me. I said, "I don't like it, send it back." That is what I was told.

My mother just smiled as she looked at my sister. "I'm sorry Norma, but I can't send her back. She is your baby sister, and she's not it. Her name is Adelin."

My mom said, Norma just sit on that chair and relax. You will hold Adelin, and you will love her....

Throughout the years my sister and I would fight with each other, but it was also throughout these same years that it became clear that I was there to protect her.

So, two-year-old me was made fun of by other family members because Adelin was there. I was so used on getting all the attention. Now, no one looked after me.

My sister and I were getting bigger and bigger. Unlike my sister, I was so outgoing, I never stopped talking. When it was time for her to go to school we rode on the same bus. We attended P.S.169, in Brooklyn, NY.

I had to deal with bullies on that bus because they used to pick on us. I always kept fighting to keep her safe. We slowly began to understand each other. I knew that my main job was to always help Adelin. My only friend....

Chapter 9

Growing up in Puerto Rico

As years went by, I grew to be a very responsible young lady. I was always ready to help my siblings...

By the end of 1954, my family was expanding. I had two brothers and one sister. My mother needed help from her mother and the in-laws, but that wasn't enough.

Since I was the oldest, I had to work extremely hard to help my mother. Both of my grandmothers, Guadalupe and Ceferina taught me how to cook and clean. I even invented my own recipes with the help of my great-grandmother Mama Dolores.

By 1959, my parents had bought a larger house still close to my grandparents. We were happy...

I spend a lot of time playing with my sister Adelin. When Juan was learning how to walk, Julio was learning how to eat rice and beans.

I played a lot with other relatives. My aunts and uncles, on my father's side, were close to my age. I was always laughing because my uncles tried to teach me boys stuff and my aunts were trying to teach me how to play with dolls.

I remember one time that my aunt Ana Dolores and I begged Mama Lupe to give us a chicken coop. There were a couple of them around the backyard. They kept lots of hens and roosters.

So, since my grandmother was always busy sewing or cooking, she was not really listening to us. She told us to take any of them and to leave her work in peace.

We ran outside and started cleaning the place up. I swept while my aunt went inside the house to get small chairs and a table that Papá Julio made for us. The furniture looked great.

We placed the cute little chairs with a table in a corner. My uncle Villen got rugs and Moncho started painting the outside of the tiny house. It was beginning to look like a real doll house.

My other aunt Lucy was already living in New York, but we told her that we would take care of her dolls.

As soon as the doll house was finished, we all stepped out to admire our work. We all agreed that we made a masterpiece.

My uncle Kike did not know about our project neither my father. They came home with some chickens and did not tell anyone. It was getting dark, and my father took me home....

The following day, Adelin and I got up exceedingly early. We were going to bring our favorite toys to the doll house. My mother gave us more pillows and dishes she did not need.

When Adelin and I went to my grandmother's house we got very angry. We found my aunt Ana Dolores crying. Moncho and Villen were also very upset. The chickens that my father and Kike brought the night before destroyed everything. There were bird drops all around the tiny house.

My grandmother had the nerves to scold us. She told us that we had no business making a doll house of a chicken cage. We reminded her that we got her permission to use anything we wanted in the backyard.

My grandmother apologized and asked my father and uncles to make us a real doll house. This time we even got our own blueprints for the house. It was beautiful. My grandfather cleaned the furniture and once again Villen and Moncho painted everything.

My aunt Lolin, Adelin and I made sandwiches and lemonade to celebrate the opening doors of our new doll house. It was really a job well done...

Life was going great for the Pagán family, however, Juan wanted more. He was in the National Guard and had an excellent job with the government. What he really wanted was to go abroad.

He kept talking about it and the whole family insisted that he didn't have to leave our beautiful island, Puerto Rico.

Chapter 10

The Visit September 1959

On one late autumn afternoon, we had a surprise visit from my mother's side of the family. It was her oldest brother, Pedro Morales Figueroa. He came for a short visit from New York. He was happy to see everyone.

When my uncle was about to go home. So, my father decided to talk to him. My uncle listened very carefully. He told my dad that it was a great idea to move to New York. My father was still in the National Guard and was a licensed plumber. He was prepared to work anywhere.

My parents did not hesitate to make the big move. They thought about their four children. Since we were still incredibly young, we would not have any problem learning a second language. I must admit that I was quite excited when I heard the good news.

All of us were asking plenty of questions. The best one was about the plane ride....

On September 9, 1959, my parents packed our bags and told us that my uncle Kike was going to drive one car and another family member another one....

During that time, there was not a highway from Ponce to San Juan. We had to take the old road all the way to the airport. The car that my uncle borrowed was a convertible. My uncle Villen, Moncho and Kike were happy to be with us until the last minute. It was a nice trip to the airport.

My uncle Kike just got his driver's license; therefore, he was flying through those streets. We enjoyed the ride very much, but when we got to the airport, my parents and grandmother started yelling at my uncle Kike for speeding. He got scolded badly.

It was so sad saying goodbye to Mamá Lupe and the rest of the family. They stood at the gate until we were on the plane.

Once on the plane, my father was upset because the flight attendant wanted to put us on different sections of the plane. My dad told the young lady that we had tickets with seat numbers.

Each of us had our own seat. The reason for the misunderstanding was that the flight was overbooked. There were people with the same seat numbers. It took a while for us to get seated together, but we did it.

It was hard to sleep due to the movement of the plane. The old ladies took out their rosaries and started praying. At that point I was very scared. I thought that we were going to die.

Chapter 11

New York City

Puerto Rican culture in New York

B efore I begin this chapter, I want to bring some history in my story because I believe it is important.

As soon as the Puerto Rican got to New York City, they began to form their own small "Barrios", in The Bronx, Brooklyn and in East Harlem, which would become known as Spanish Harlem.

It was in East Harlem where the Puerto Ricans established a cultural life of great vitality and sociality. Many participated in some of the sports, such as boxing and baseball. This is interesting because those sports were first introduced in the island by the American Armed Forces right after the Spanish American War.

Puerto Ricans who moved to New York took with them more than their customs and traditions. They took with them their famous "piraguas". A "piragua is a Puerto Rican frozen treat, shaped like a pyramid, made of shaved ice, and covered with fruit flavored syrup.

According to Holding Aloft, the Banner of Ethiopia, by Winston James, "piraguas" were introduced in New York by Puerto Ricans as early as 1926.

Our talented Puerto Rican musicians and singers:

At "El Teatro Puerto Rico"......

Our Puerto Rican music flourished with the likes of Rafael Hernández and Pedro Flores who formed the "Trio Borincano". It gained recognition in New York City.

Let's not forget Myrta Silva who later joined Hernandez's "Cuarteto Victoria". She also gained fame as a singer after the group traveled and played throughout the United States.

The South Bronx became the main core for the Puerto Rican music. The theaters which had served to previous groups of immigrants, such as the Irish and the Italians, for their dramatic works or vaudeville style shows, now served the growing Puerto Rican and Latino population.

The musical performances from musicians from Puerto Rico and Lat-in America made an enormous difference in New York City. Families used to travel from all boroughs to the historical "Teatro Puerto Rico" located at E. 138th Street and Hunts Point in the Bronx.

The Teatro Puerto Rico's "golden era" lasted from 1947 to 1956. This is also the place where our dear musician José Feliciano made his stateside debut.

New York City became the center for freestyle music in the 1980s, of which Puerto Rican singer-songwriters represented a fundamental component.

Puerto Rican influence in popular music continues in the 21st century, surrounding major artists such as Jennifer Lopez.

The third great wave of domestic migration from Puerto Rico came after World War II. 40,000 Puerto Ricans settled in New York City in 1946 and 58,500 in 1952–53. Many soldiers who returned after World War II made use of the GI Bill and went to college.

For the Puerto Rican women, things were horrible in New York. They confronted economic exploitation, discrimination, racism, and the insecurities inherent in the migration process daily.

Let me point out that even with the so many hardships, the women fared better than the men in the job market. The women left their homes for the factories in record numbers.

By 1953, Puerto Rican migration to New York reached its peak when 75,000 people left the island.......

Politics in the island and New York

In 1948, Puerto Ricans elected their first governor Luis Muñoz Marín, who together with his government initiated a series of social and economic reforms with the introduction of innovative programs in the is-land. Some of these programs met some resistance from the American government and therefore, the local government had some trouble implementing the same.

New York Mayor Robert F. Wagner, Jr. began a campaign to recruit Puerto Rican laborers in the island to work in the city's factories. Mayor Wagner figured that the city would benefit by the luring of what was "cheap labor".

Discrimination was widespread in the United States, and it was no different in New York. As stated by Lolita Lebron, there were signs in restaurants which read "No dogs or Puerto Ricans allowed".

The Puerto Rican Nationalist Party established an office in New York in 1950 and attracted many migrants. Leaders of the party conceived a plan that would involve an attack on the Blair House with the intention of assassinating United States President Harry S. Truman and an attack on the House of Representatives.

These events had a negative impact on the Puerto Rican. Americans viewed Puerto Ricans as anti-Americans and the discrimination against them became even more widespread.

Many Puerto Ricans were able to overcome these obstacles and became respected members of their communities.

Among those respected member in the Puerto Rican community was Antonia Pantoja. She established organizations such as "ASPIRA" that helped many compatriots to reach their goals.

The first New York Puerto Rican Day Parade was held on Sunday, April 12, 1958 in "El Barrio" located in Manhattan. Its first President was Victor Lopez, and it was coordinated by José Caballero. The grand marshal was Oscar González Suarez.

There were many personalities from Puerto Rico present in that first parade. Even Luis Munoz Marin, the governor, was present.

The parade was organized to show Puerto Rican pride and its traditions. The parade continues today in the city of New York. Let me tell you that it is also extended to other cities such as Chicago, Illinois and Orlando, Florida.

By 1960, the United States census showed that there were well over 600,000 New Yorkers of Puerto Rican birth or paternity. Estimates were that more than one million Puerto Ricans had migrated during that period.

<u>Nuyorican Movement</u>

The Nuyorican Poets Café......

Puerto Rican writer Jesús Colón founded an intellectual movement involving poets, writers, musicians, and artists who are Puerto Rican or of Puerto Rican descent. They lived in or near New York City. Those people, which I admire, became known as the Nuyorican Movement.

The phenomenon of the "Nuyoricans" came about when many Puerto Ricans who migrated to New York City faced tricky situations and hardships, such as racial discrimination.

Who is a "Nuyorican"? He or she is a simple Puerto Rican which developed a subculture.

In 1980, Puerto Rican poets Miguel Algarín, Miguel Piñero and Pedro Pietri established the "Nuyorican Poets Café". It is Located on

Manhattan's Lower East Side 236 E 3rd Street, between Avenues B and C. This is now considered a New York landmark.

By 1964, the Puerto Rican community made up 9.3 percent of the total New York City's population. The Puerto Rican migrants who gained economic success began to move away from "El Barrios" and settled mostly in Westchester County or moved to other states.

At the present time, new immigrants from the Dominican Republic, Mexico and South America moved into the "Barrios". The Puerto Ricans once mainly occupied this area.

In the 1970s we saw what became known as reverse-migration. Many Puerto Ricans returned to the island to buy homes. Puerto Ricans returned to Puerto Rico to invest in local businesses.

I want to point out that Puerto Ricans have made many important contributions to New York and the society of the United States in general. They have contributed to the fields of entertainment, the arts, music, industry, science, politics, and the armed forces.

Since 2006, there has been recovery in migration from Puerto Rico to New York City and New Jersey. Apparently, multifactorial ap-pealed to Puerto Ricans. It was primarily for economic and cultural considerations. The Census estimated for the New York City has in-creased from 723,621 in 2010, to 730,848 in 2012.

New York State overall has also resumed its net in-migration of Puerto Rican Americans since 2006. New York was the only state to register a decrease in its Puerto Rican population between 1990 and 2000. The Puerto Rican population of New York State still is the largest in the United States. It is estimated by the U.S. Census Bureau to have increased from 1,070,558 in 2010 to 1,103,067 in 2013.

New York State gained more Puerto Rican migrants from Puerto Rico as well as from elsewhere on the mainland between 2006 and 2012 than any other state in absolute numbers.

Also, unlike the initial pattern of migration several decades ago, this second Puerto Rican migration into New York is being driven by movement not only into New York City, but also into the city's surrounding suburban areas. New York City Metropolitan area gained the highest number of additional Puerto Rican Americans of any metropolitan area between 2010 and 2013.

As Puerto Ricans continue to climb the socioeconomic ladder and achieve a greater degree of professional occupations, the community is also purchasing homes in New Jersey's more affluent suburban towns.

Puerto Rican migration patterns, 1995-2000

Brooklyn has several neighborhoods with a Puerto Rican presence. Many of the ethnic Puerto Rican neighborhoods in Brooklyn were formed before the Puerto Rican neighborhoods in the South Bronx because of the work demand in the Brooklyn Navy Yard in the 1940s and 50s.

Bushwick has the highest concentration of Puerto Ricans in Brooklyn New York, Brownsville, Coney Island, Red Hook, and Sunset Park.

In Williamsburg, Graham Avenue is nicknamed "Avenue of Puerto Rico" because of the high density and strong ethnic territory of Puerto Ricans who have been living in the neighborhood since the 1950s.

The Puerto Rican day parade is also hosted on the avenue....

Puerto Rican neighborhoods in Manhattan included Spanish Harlem and Loisaida. Spanish Harlem was "Italian Harlem" from the 1880s until the 1940s.

By 1940, however, the name "Spanish Harlem" was becoming wide-spread, and by 1950, the area was predominately Puerto Rican and African American.

Let us look at Loisaida

Loisaida is a district on the east of Avenue A. That district originally consisted of German, Jewish, Irish, and Italian working-class residents. They lived in tenements without running water; the German presence, already in decline, virtually ended after the General Slocum disaster in 1904.

Since then, the community has become Puerto Rican and Latino in character, despite the "gentrification" that has affected the East Village and the Lower East Side since the late 20th century.

Staten Island has a large Puerto Rican population along the North Shore, especially in the Mariners' Harbor, Arlington, Elm Park, Graniteville, Port Richmond, and Stapleton neighborhoods, where the population is 20%.

In New York and many other cities, Puerto Ricans usually live in proximity with other Latinos and African Americans. There is also a large concentration of Puerto Ricans present in public housing developments throughout the city.

Puerto Ricans are present in large numbers throughout the Bronx. The Bronx has the highest percentage of Puerto Ricans of any borough. In some places in the South Bronx, Spanish is the primary language.

Throughout the 1970s, the South Bronx became known as the essence of a town weakening but has since made a recovery.

Puerto Rican population in New York keeps increasing.......

As of 1990, New Yorkers of Puerto Rican descent, Nuyoricans, numbered 143,974. Nearly 41,800 state residents Nuyoricans in 1990 had lived in Puerto Rico in 1985.

According to the Census taken in the year 2000, Puerto Rican migrants make up a 1.2% of the total population of the United States with a population of well over 3 million Puerto Ricans including those of Puerto Rican descent.

You must keep in mind that we are U.S. citizens. We shall never be excluded by the U.S. Census statistics of U.S. population.

We make up about 2.5% of the total population of U.S. citizens around the world. I am talking about the inside and outside the U.S. mainland.

In July 1930, Puerto Rico's Department of Labor established an employment service in New York City....

The Migration Division known as the "Commonwealth Office", also part of Puerto Rico's Department of Labor, was created in 1948, and by the end of the 1950s, was operating in one hundred and fifteen cities.

The Department of Puerto Rican Affairs in the United States was established in 1989 as a cabinet-level department in Puerto Rico.

Currently, the Commonwealth operates the Puerto Rico Federal Affairs Administration, which is headquartered in Washington, D.C. and has twelve regional offices throughout the United States.

Puerto Ricans in New York have preserved their cultural heritage by being involved actively in the different political and social rights movements in the United States. They founded "Aspira", a leader in the field of education, in 1961.

When I was in high school, I used to work in an afternoon program funded by Aspira. My job was to teach writing skills to Puerto Ricans young adults. It helped many teenagers score high in the S.A.T's.

Let me tell you that Aspira still is one of the largest national Latino nonprofit organizations in the United States.

There are other educational and social organizations founded by Puerto Ricans in New York. I am proud to say that I worked in the National Puerto Rican Forum from 1985 thru 1994. I started as an English Instructor. I was promoted to Head Instructor in 1986.

The reason I left that wonderful institution was that I was offered a job as an English teacher in the public school system.

Now let me return to my relocation to New York....

September 10, 1959......

We got to New York City at about 4:00 a.m. yet, it was very dark and so ugly. When we got off the plane, I started to cry. Adelin and the boys kept their mouth shut. They really had no idea of the whole situation. They were just confused.

That autumn day on September 10, 1959, was the very same day that the Department of Sanitation in New York was on strike. There was garbage everywhere. The smell was nasty that I started thinking about Puerto Rico.

I had flashbacks of my room full of stuffed animals and the books my grandfather gave me. I just cried in silence because I didn't want my parents to know how sad I was. I left behind more than material things.

I left behind so many people that really loved me. My grandfather, Julio, didn't say goodbye. He didn't know that he wouldn't see us ever again.

My parents had other problems. We really didn't have a place to live. It wasn't easy finding a five-room apartment.

My dear uncle Pedro Morales and his family tried very hard to help. They told my parents not to worry. My uncle had a plan. He informed my mother that there was one solution. The plan was to separate the family. We had to live with different family members. Adelin and I stayed with my uncle Pedro and the boys went to live with my parents in another part of Brooklyn with my uncle Ruben.

You know I really enjoyed living with my cousins in the projects. We were one big happy family.

My father had an education, a good job and earned enough money to raise a family in Puerto Rico, therefore, he had no problem in New York. It didn't take long for him to find a job and at the same time an apartment.

Still, I wasn't happy. In school, I told Adelin not to speak English. My plan was to stay quiet so that we can be sent to Puerto Rico.

One morning, while in school, my cousin was called to my classroom to translate something, because my teacher couldn't get any information from Adelin or me.

When my 4th grade teacher, Mrs. Kramer, spoke to my cousin, I started to laugh. I began speaking in English. The teacher was surprised because I expressed myself very well.

Chapter 12

First Christmas in New York

C hildren have much vivid imagination to forget about bad experiences at home or in school....

The following chapter will indicate how I managed to forget about my environment by just imagining things...

I was only ten when I first saw him. I remember that switch from one situation around my surroundings to the other. I used to have imaginary friends and it worked fine for a while....

I used to make believe that I will get help from God. Why did I think like that? Well, to begin with when I had an assignment, I did it with no problem.

I remember one day so clearly. It was right after school started in September 1959, my first week in school in New York....

Many people came to see the apartment on the second floor, but they said that it was too small for their family.

On that autumn day of 1959, I just knew that the man that took the apartment was going to be my friend. He wasn't too tall, and his hair was white and long. He also had a close-cropped white beard.

By the way, the lady next door smiled when she saw him. I guessed he must have reminded her of someone from yesteryears. He was carrying a box; it was marked "early birds" on its side.

There were some moving men helping him. He was very busy all day long. Some neighbors wanted to know what he did for a living, but no one even dared to ask him.

Two weeks went by and as it did, I watched the new tenant very closely. I'd hear him in his apartment listening to music, TV, and talking. I never got close enough to hear what was said in his living room, but we shared a wall between our kitchens.

One day, mom caught Adelin and me with a glass against my ear. I put the glass very close on the wall trying to hear the conversation next door. Boy: did we get into trouble for that!

We were grounded for three days. That was the punishment for ease-dropping, as mom called it. Adelin didn't want to play detective with me. She didn't want any part of my games. My brothers were too small to know about the games.

So, I was on my own....

The next day, I ran into my new neighbor after my three days of punishment. He was coming in as I was going out. I was hurrying and just as I jumped from the second step of the stairs, he came in through the front door, and we crashed together. He fell backwards but as he did, he caught me and saved me from falling.

The door slammed into his back, and I heard him grunt from it hitting him. I just knew I'd be in more trouble, so as soon as he let me go, I started apologizing like crazy. He stood there for a minute, then raised his hand chuckling. I thought he was going to hit me!

Instead, he said, whoa, slow down young lady... it's not a problem. I would have done the same thing if I were your age. Then... he started laughing. "In fact," he said, "I have done it in my younger days". I asked him, "Are you going to tell me? My mom will kill me if you do. He smiled and said, no, it's our secret, you don't tell, I won't tell.

He told me that his name was Mr. Reilly. I found it strange that he didn't tell me his first name. It didn't matter. I always use last names with people not related to me....

After a couple of days, Mr. Reilly offered me a job; he paid me to take out his trash. He would sit it outside his door every other morning, and I would take it on my way out to school. He paid me five dollars a week. My parents thought it was too much, but he insisted. I thought to myself that Mr. Reilly was a cool guy.

He was a little overweight and older than my parents......

I was so curious about Mr. Reilly. He always had some visitors, which I never saw coming or leaving. Some of them only stayed for maybe an hour. I was just guessing. This Mr. Nice Guy may be a spy.

I was also very puzzled by the end of October because I didn't know what Mr. Reilly did as far as work. I began to guess again. He was maybe a secret agent or something. He didn't work hours like my father or Mr. Alvarez in apartment 2B.

I noticed he was home when I got home from school, and he was there when I left in the morning. Sometimes he was gone for two or three days, but he still paid me the five dollars even if I only took his trash out once that week.

One day, I overheard him talking to someone inside his place. It appeared he was upset about something. I heard the other man say that it wasn't his fault. He also stated that it would be ready on time. I could tell he was nervous, and then they came out.

They stopped in the hall in front of Mr. Reilly apartment. They closed the door as they left. I heard Mr. Reilly say something about being disappointed, and they left the building.

I tried to figure out what the whole deal meant, but it was over my head. The visitor was small like me. I think they call people like that midget. He was dressed funny; in clothes no one wore in my neighborhood.

After that incident, I started pretending I was a secret agent, and it was my job to spy on the other spies especially the one who lived next door...

Things went back to normal after Mr. Reilly settled down. Since he didn't visit anyone that lived in our building, it was kind of boring spying on him. I knew better than to try listening again through the wall. If I got caught again by my mom, I would be grounded forever.

One afternoon, it dawned on me that I had never seen the inside Mr. Reilly's apartment. I asked Adelin to take a walk with me. Adelin, so shy said, "No. I don't want to get in trouble." She claimed that Christmas was around the corner, and she wanted nice presents.

I was still determined to see Mr. Reilly's apartment. I thought I would ask him to help me with my homework. I went to his door, and as I was about to knock, I heard, come-in young lady, it's open. I don't know how he knew that it was me, but I did as he said.

As I walked in, he was sitting at a desk. I noticed it was only one of three pieces of furniture in the room. He had a TV, a couch, a desk, and a chair. On the desk there were letters, lots, and lots of letters. I couldn't see who they were from.

Mr. Reilly had gotten up from the desk and met me before I could get close enough to see. He smiled at me and said, "So; you need help with your homework, do you?"

Surprised, I asked... how do you know? He smiled again; his eyes seemed to sparkle as he did. It made me feel like everything was okay; it made me forget he knew beforehand.

Why aren't you out riding your bike, he asked? I don't have a bike, I answered. The next thing I knew, and I was leaving his apartment with my homework and completed.

When I returned to my apartment, I looked at the clock over the TV; one and a half hours had passed, and all I remembered was we had done my homework. That's when I knew Mr. Reilly was someone special.

In mid-November, there was a big argument between Mr. and Mrs. Rentas, up in apartment 3A. It started out kind of easy with only one word. Then it got louder until finally everyone in the building heard it. My parents told me I wasn't allowed to go upstairs.

I wanted to go and see them fight, but my mother said if I put one foot on those stairs, I would be grounded for a month. So, I just stood at the stairway.

Then, everything got very quiet, and I heard…"It isn't nice to find pleasure in another's misery." I turned around and looking at me with the happiest smile was Mr. Reilly. He said, 'excuse me,' and then he stepped passed me and went upstairs.

A few minutes later, I heard a door close. Then, Mr. Reilly came down smiling more than before. He went to his apartment without saying a word. Mr. and Mrs. Rentas had stopped fighting.

There was no yelling or fighting. All that I could hear was the normal sounds of pipes rattling, people walking, and other normal sounds of a three-story brick apartment building.

Two days before Thanksgiving, my parents sent my sister and me to Mr. Reilly's apartment. They wanted to invite him to our Thanksgiving's dinner.

They said they didn't know if he had plans. My parents thought that it would be nice to have him. It would also be the neighborly thing to do.

So, I went next door…

I knocked and stood waiting for him to say come in. I waited and a few minutes went by, and we knocked again. Still there was no answer. I decided to try the door and to my surprise it was unlocked.

As I pushed it open, I said, "Mr. Reilly? Are you here?" When he didn't answer, I opened the door more and stepped inside.

By this time, I decided to look around the apartment. As I did, I noticed everything seemed the same from the last time I was there. The only difference was that there weren't any letters on the desk.

I was concentrating on my investigation. I saw now that there was a roll of paper with names lying there. I was just about to reach for it when I heard, "It's not polite to invite ones self-inside another's home!" I jumped about two feet then turned around. There, smiling as always, was Mr. Reilly, eyes twinkling.

Well young lady: "Do you have a message for me?" I just stood there, embarrassed. "Well?" He spoke. I stared at him for a moment then remembered why I had gone to his apartment; oh yeah, I started talking.

My parents wanted me to invite you to our house for Thanksgiving's dinner. Mr. Reilly's smile widened, and he replied, tell your parents that I would be happy to join your family on that special holiday. He also asked me if he needed to bring anything. It was my turn to smile; only your appetite I replied.

Thanksgiving Day

Mom brushed off her apron as she went to answer the door. I was busy mashing potatoes, and my sister was setting the table when we heard the knock. "Am I too early?" I heard Mr. Reilly say after Mom opened the door. "Goodness No!" You're just in time, my father replied with joy. The boys were playing, and I was finishing mashing potatoes.

As I walked into the living room, I felt very happy. My brothers and my parents were talking to Mr. Reilly. Then Mr. Reilly said, "Oh… I almost forgot" Mr. Reilly handed dad a paper bag with something inside.

My father pulled out what looked like a bottle of wine, and stated, now Mr. Reilly, you didn't have to do this. I guess I kind of frowned because Mr. Reilly smiled at me and said to my father, it isn't wine, its Sparkling cider, these young children are too young to drink.

Also, I don't indulge myself. We walked to the table where Mom asked my sister and me to help bring the remaining items from the kitchen. The boys were happy to sit next to Mr. Reilly. My father sat at the head of the table and my mom beside him.

My sister and I were sitting side by side. Our Thanksgiving dinner wasn't anything special; Mom had baked a small turkey which she bought on special. We had mashed potatoes, rice, pageant peas, green salad, stuffing, and cranberry sauce. For dessert Mom had made a pumpkin pie topped with a cool whip.

After dinner, Mr. Reilly helped clean up and then he offered to wash the dishes. My first thought was alright! No dishes for me tonight, but as usual, I was wrong. Mom told Mr. Reilly guest don't do dishes in our home, "do they my dear daughter?" Knowing what was next, I said no, and I went to the kitchen with Adelin and started the water.

My parents and Mr. Reilly talked for a while then I heard him say, you must let me supply Christmas dinner and with that he left…

December came and with it, all the songs, commercials, and billboards. My dad was working two jobs by now. The money was just to pay the rent and bills. My parents had enough money to get us a present and a tree. I already knew we wouldn't have much, but we were used to it.

Christmas was never my favorite time of the year because I saw how it bothered my parents. They didn't feel comfortable in New York as they did in Puerto Rico. Money was very tight.

During the next few days, I saw Mr. Reilly often. He was either coming or going to his apartment. On the first Friday of the month, he had pinned an envelope to his trash, it just said "READ THIS". Inside was a note that read, I'm sure you'll need this before Christmas, consider it an advance pay for the month.

Attached was a twenty-dollar bill. The note was written in red ink. After that I rarely saw Mr. Reilly. I saw the midgets several times during the next two weeks, but Mr. Reilly only once.

A couple of days before Christmas, Mr. Reilly was on his way out, with a big suit bag like those used when traveling. I asked him what was in it, he looked at me and with a sly smile, replied, "Why, my Santa suit of course!" then he started chuckling. I just thought he was being a wise guy and smiled back. He continued walking down the hall humming jingle bells as he did.

Two days before Christmas, I saw Mr. and Mrs. Rentas carrying groceries into the building. They never looked happier. Mrs. Rentas whispered softly to her husband as they walked.

All the neighbors heard Mrs. Rentas told them that her husband had stopped drinking. He was even working and helping around the house.

On Christmas Eve, my father sent me to ask Mr. Reilly if he wanted to join us for some "coquito" and "arroz con dulce".

I knocked and knocked, but he didn't answer. I put my ear to the door and listened but heard nothing. I went back and told my parents that he wasn't home.

When I returned to our apartment, Mr. and Mrs. Rentas stopped by, then, Mr. Rodriguez and the Smith family showed up.

Next thing we knew, there were several people at our tiny apartment talking, and drinking "coquito". Mr. Rodriguez took out a guitar and started playing "parranda" songs, slowly, everybody started singing.

I couldn't help but wish Mr. Reilly was here too. It was almost midnight when everyone left. My parents and I picked up the glasses and took them to the kitchen.

Mom told us to leave everything in the sink. She to us that all the dishes would be cleaned in the morning.

I filled the sink with dish washing detergent. I placed the glasses and small dishes in the sink. I went back into the living room with my father. Adelin and the boys have been sleeping for a couple of hours by now. They went to sleep early so that Christmas morning would get here faster.

Our tree was only about two feet tall, but it was beautiful. We all helped with the decoration. My father let each one of us put on the tinsel and decoration while he did the lights.

We stood still, in the living room looking at the tree; there were only seven presents under it. Each of us had one gift from my parents.

I got one for Mr. Reilly. I looked up at my parents and they were smiling at me. They knew that I was thinking about Puerto Rico, but still, love filled the room...

On Christmas morning, I woke up hearing my parent's saying, "Oh my goodness!" I quickly rushed into the living room and couldn't believe my eyes. The tree we had only the night before had grown.

It was an easy six feet tall, fully decorated and sparkling like it was covered with stars. Underneath it there were presents lots and lots of presents.

In the dining room, the table was filled with food, ham, turkey, and dressing. There were all kinds of food. Even Christmas cookies. My parents were amazed. Where did it all come from, they whispered.

We looked at each other and, at the same time said, "What happened?" I started to reach for one of the many gifts when I saw a note tied to a branch of the tree. I pulled it off and looked at it; all that was written on it was, "To the Pagán family".

I handed it to Mom and waited as she opened it. I watched as she silently read the note inside.

Tears welled up in her eyes and started rolling down her face. Mom, what is it, I asked. She looked at me and smiled, she handed me the note and I read, Merry Christmas.

It was signed with S. Nicholas. Who is this person, I asked. My Parents smiled again and said, the answer is found with the gifts. Each gift was signed by your friend, S. Nicholas.

Who is S. Nicholas I asked again? My father reached down, picked up a gift wrapped in shiny red wrapping paper, here, he said to my sister and maybe this one will answer your question. There wasn't a name tag on it. She quickly ripped it open, and inside she found a Barbie doll.

Adelin longed for that doll for years. In the box was a note, it said, "It isn't polite to question a gift origin", Love, Mr. Reilly. You may know me better as Saint Nicholas or Santa for short.

That was one great Christmas morning, even though we were far away from Puerto Rico. This story, my friends, was just a dream…

Chapter 13

New Year 1960

January 1960, Adelin, and I were ready for Public School 169…
You know, I found out that not only the education was better at our new school, but also the teachers. We made friends right away. I became class president and tutor to some of my classmates.

So many years have gone by, and I still think of my precious island.

My grandfather, Julio Pagan Torres died on October 10, 1964, and my great-grandmother in June 1972. Guadalupe was left alone. She sold her house, in Ponce, and moved to New York.

I was a bit happy because I could be with all my uncles and aunts. My grandmother Guadalupe taught me more stuff. I learned how to sew my own clothing and my cooking was superb!

I graduated from Prospect Heights High School and was accepted at Colombia University where I studied Criminal Justice. I am also qualified to work in the New York City Police Department. I was happy because I have accomplished a lot.

While in the Police Department, I met what I thought was the love of my life, a Police Officer. He was really a "Latin Lover". He didn't speak Spanish at all. I made so much fun of him.

As we started dating, he didn't like the idea of having a chaperone. He was born in New York and his upbringing was different from mine. He had so many girlfriends that I guessed he only came to visit me because he liked my cooking.

Our little romance lasted only a few months because I informed him that I wasn't part of his dolls' collection. I wished him well and that was the end of it.

I kept working in the Police Department and I also kept studying. Adelin followed my footsteps. Right after graduating from high school, she started Brooklyn College. She got a great job with the federal government.

The minute I graduated from the University; I knew was ready for a vacation. I couldn't believe that after almost twenty years I was finally going to my island.

My mother started making plans. She wanted to see her family, and this was a good chance to do so. Adelin and my friend Beverly also wanted to go with me. I was happy to return to Puerto Rico with Adelin and mom.

I couldn't sleep all night. I just wanted to be on that plane to see a few cousins and my grandmother Ceferina Figueroa Bello.

Chapter 14

Returning to Puerto Rico 1972

The flight was great. We were greeted at the airport by some of my relatives. My uncle Kike, as always, was waiting for us. He didn't want to miss the opportunity of seeing my first reaction as we were heading towards Ponce.

Everything was so different. Now there is a highway. The trip to the south part of Puerto Rico is more enjoyable. The scenery is awesome.

 My cousins kept asking us about the rest of the family in New York. We just kept talking and told them many events that had happened to each family member.

We got to Ponce about 3 p.m. without a problem. Our first hour was spent unpacking a handing out gifts. It was great seeing my cousins on the Pagán side of the family.

Kike was the only one that didn't relocate to New York. He had a good job in P.R. He and his wife Migdalia were happy raising their three children. Life for them was great on the island.

The following day we got up early and went to see my grandmother Ceferina. My mother was anxious to see Mamá Nina. She was living with my Aunt Emma and her family.

When we got to "Jardines Del Caribe", Lourdes and her two brothers were waiting for us. Right away they told us that we were going dancing that night.

The dance was going to take place at the university which they were attending. I informed them that I wanted to meet a guy from the university. I also stated that he should have the same interests as me.

My aunt was quite happy to see us. She made a great feast on our behalf. My grandmother Ceferina was all smiles when she saw all of us sitting at the dining table.

After eating a big lunch, we started making plans for the evening. I told my cousin Angel that I was ready for that great dance. He laughed when I reminded him that I was searching for a husband.

When we got to the dance, it was hard to get a table. The place was packed. The music was blasting. I didn't mind having a table because I went there to dance. I never sit during a dance or party.

At the dance

I danced with a lot of my cousin's friends. They were very polite. These guys were so different from the ones I met in New York City.

When the dance was almost over, I asked my cousin about the young man I was going to meet. My cousin laughed. He was here; however, he saw you dancing and left without saying a word.

We got to my aunt's house about 2 a.m. My mother and aunt were up. They wanted to hear about our adventure. They both enjoyed listening to us. We told them that we really had a great time. As always, Tía Emma made sandwiches and coffee. We ate and went to sleep.

The following day, we all got up at about 11 a.m. I was well rested. I was walking around in my pajamas when my cousin informed that the so call mystery young man was coming to meet me during lunch.

I just looked at Angel and told him to forget it. I wasn't planning on going out or fixing myself up for some fool that didn't bother to talk to me during the dance. My cousin told me that it was too late. The young man was parking his car in front of the house.

Well, too late to get dressed and impress a fool. I sat with my hair in curlers. I had no makeup on and still with my pajamas. I was too busy eating an "asopao de pollo" that my aunt made. I didn't even look up to see this guy.

He pulled a chair and sat across from me. He introduced himself. My name is Eliezer Ramos, your future husband. I started laughing so hard that I was shocked.

He also said that I looked good with no makeup and wearing my pajamas. Believe it was a funny sight.

I was very impressed by this young man. He spoke English with no accent whatsoever. He told me that he was a senior at the Catholic University of Ponce. He wanted to be a doctor. He also told me about his hobbies and that he enjoyed the beach and all water sports.

We spoke for a couple of hours. I even forgot that at 3 p.m. I was still with my pajamas talking to a total stranger. I excused myself, took a shower and got dressed.

I put on a pair of white shorts, and a short blue sleeves blouse. I wore a nice pair of sandals. My hair was very long so I just made a ponytail. I wasn't ready to impress this guy that saw me earlier in my pjs…

As I walked into the living room, he just kept looking at me. I asked him what was wrong with my outfit. He said I looked gorgeous. I just smiled. He informed me that we were going out that night. I reminded him that it doesn't work like that.

He was supposed to ask me first and if I agreed, we would go out that night. He apologized and asked me if I would like to go for a drive and perhaps a movie.

I told him sure, but that my cousins were going with me. He said that he was expecting that.

Before we went off to the movies, he told me that he wanted me to meet two of his friends. My cousin Lourdes was smiling when we reached a house located a couple of blocks from my family.

I got out of the car and found it very strange that no one greeted us. He went into the house as if he was the owner. He told us to sit in the living room and we did. I looked at my cousin Lourdes because she still had that grin I didn't like.

Suddenly, my mystery man walked into the living room with an elderly couple. I was very puzzled. He said to them, "Papí, Mamí, esta es mi novia Norma".

I was in a state of shock. This fool introduced me to his parents as his girlfriend. They both smiled and were very pleased to meet me. Then an older sister, Delia, also came out to meet me.

She was so happy because her younger brother had a girlfriend. Delia asked him what our plans were for the evening. He told her about the drive-in movie and then sightseeing around Ponce.

Delia didn't hesitate in giving her brother her car keys. Her car was a super beetle. It was brand new!

The movie was great… it was Love Story…

After the movie, we went for some ice-cream and for a walk around "la Plaza"….

The next day, he came for breakfast. My cousin invited him without telling me. I was already used to the idea of everyone trying to hook me up with this guy. As the day before, he saw me in my pjs…

We ate breakfast; however, this time even my grandma, Ceferina, joined us. I guessed she was also in this matching adventure.

Time was going very fast…. I was getting so used to the idea of seeing this guy. I had to return to New York. I was counting the days, the hours, and minutes. I must leave my island once again….

As we were heading towards the airport, Eliezer held my hand and said, "I am going to New York, and we are going to get married". I must admit, I didn't want to leave him. I don't know if I was used to him or that I really cared for him.

The whole family took us to the airport…

When I got to New York, I was a completely different person. My parents asked me what was wrong with me. I told them that I miss Puerto Rico. I didn't go into details about meeting my future husband.

Eliezer called me at least three times a week. I wrote to him. Communication in 1972 wasn't that easy. The calls were expensive.

On September 1972, Eliezer told me that he was moving to New York. He was going to stay with his brother Eliot.

The minute Eliezer arrived, he decided to go for a job interview. Adelin helped him with the application. He was applying for a job with the U.S. Government, Food and Drugs Administration.

Adelín introduced Eliezer to the head of that department. He took the test and within weeks he was working for FDA as an Inspector.

Things were going well that in February 17, 1973, we got married. It was a beautiful wedding. The bride's mates were dressed in 18th century outfits. Those dresses were beautiful. All the girls' dresses were in burgundy, but my sister's and Ida. Their dresses were pink. They each had a parasol made of flowers.

We all had the same hairdo....long banana curls. The ushers wore long tail tux. It was a wedding straight from a fairy tale. It was also full of love.

The church was well decorated with white flowers.

My flower girl was my cousin Ada. She was only 6 yrs. old, and the ring bearer was Kermit, Eliezer's nephew.

After the church ceremony, we went to the reception hall. It was a very lovely place in Brooklyn. The food was excellent. We had a choice of chicken or roast beef, vegetables etc. The cake was three levels and very beautiful.

My grandmother made the favors and center pieces. She also made my wedding dress. Thanks to Mama Lupe it was truly a beautiful reception.

We went to the Poconos at Mount Airy Lodge, Pennsylvania for our honeymoon. It was below zero, therefore, we had all the winter sports which we enjoy practicing. We were there for one week.

When we got home, Adelin had already counted the money we received as wedding gifts. With all that money, we bought our first car.

My father was very happy because he had time to finish an apartment that he was going to rent. He told us to stay there until we had enough money to buy a house. We lived there rent free. Within a couple of months, we bought a house.

Moving day....

We found our dream house in Ozone Park, Queens NY. It was a corner house. I fell in love with it the minute I saw it. My father, brothers and friends did the moving.

We started decorating and buying furniture. Things were going great.

Eliezer was a loving husband. He was always trying to please me. We kept studying....

Days turned into weeks and then into years. We have been married for almost 5 years when we decided to have a child....

I got pregnant but had a miscarriage. I was very sad...

On that same year that I had the miscarriage, I told Eliezer that it was time to move to Puerto Rico. I wanted to return to my island. He made the necessary arrangement, and his supervisor transferred him to San Juan. I was happy once again.

We bought a house in Bayamon. It had four bedrooms, two bathrooms, a living room, dining room and a big kitchen. The backyard and garage were nice. I had a place to do my gardening. Life once again was great.

One Sunday afternoon, when we were visiting his parents, the baby topic came up. We didn't tell his family the reason I lost the baby...

Eliezer still wanted to make me happy in every possible way. I told him that I felt comfortable just being in Puerto Rico with his family and my parents.

I was in love with my husband. I didn't care if I had a child or not, however, on June 30, 1985, we were divorced.

My sister in-law Delia died just a couple of weeks before we moved to Puerto Rico. I was very sick for a while. Delia was a sweetheart. She left two children, a baby boy of 4 yrs. and a girl of only 6 months. Delia had a brain tumor and died at a very young age.

I know that if Delia would have been alive today, Eliezer and I would have survived every obstacle in life. I am sorry to say that Micaela Ramos and Adolfo Ramos, Eliezer's parents, died many years after our divorce. I will never forget them…

I keep in touch with some of Eliezer's nieces and nephews. The Ramos family was part of me and will always be….

After the divorce, in 1985, I returned to New York. I had plenty of friends which helped me get a good job teaching at the Puerto Rico National Forum. I got a beautiful apartment, bought a nice car and did well for myself.

After a couple of years at the Forum, I resigned. I took the National Teaching Examination and was certified to teach in the City of New York. The benefits were better. I loved working with children and young adults.

I also helped people living with aid. Counseling young adults about this sickness wasn't easy.

In 1994, I started working as an instructor/counselor for Housing Works. This is an organization located in Broadway and Houston in New York City. It now has lots of other offices throughout the City of New York. It was great helping my clients. Some came out of jail with nothing and were very grateful in receiving a helping hand.

For the homeless and people with Aids, this organization is heaven…

On cold weekends I always volunteered to work in soup kitchens. I used to get a couple of chickens, rice, vegetable, and plenty of beans from the Hispanic store owners. They didn't hesitate in giving us supplies of any kind because it was for a good cause.

The homeless were always waiting for their meals in front of the soup kitchen; however, when they saw me, it was different. They knew they were going to get the best lunch ever.

I enjoyed seeing them happy. Sometimes I gave them clothes and blankets. My job was really to help them get into the program at Housing Works.

Even though I was working for the Job Training Department, I was a volunteer at the library that was in the making. Housing Works Inc. receives hundreds of educational materials daily. I enjoyed classifying books and getting them ready for sale.

The good thing about the library was the way it was arranged. It was also a coffee shop; therefore, we named it Housing Works Book Store Café.

I was happy, but still I wanted to move to Puerto Rico. I was tired of the cold weather. My parents weren't doing well. My mom was sick all the time and my dad with diabetes and chronic arthritis.

Many years went by, and I still had the desire to live in my island....

On January 16, 1997, I went to Puerto Rico for a visit. My dad, who had relocated to the island back in 1980, was working for the Puerto Rico National Guard. He asked me if I wanted to work there. Right away I replied...yes!

I returned to New York and got all my documentation ready for Puerto Rico. I had a secondary teaching license and had plenty of experience. I was fully qualified for my job as an English Instructor to a second to none organization.

I moved to Puerto Rico and even with all my qualifications, I had to work for Puerto Rico board of education for at least one year. I worked as an English Teacher at "el Colegio Ponceño" for one year and then in the public school system for six months.

It wasn't easy. The kids in both schools were very poor in English. They had no respect for teachers.

I had a big problem; my Spanish was horrible. I spoke to them only in English. I informed their parents, in both schools, that speaking to their kids in English was the only way they would learn. The directors and parents agreed with me, however, the students didn't.

They told me that their previous teachers used to teach them songs. They would sing all day and had a practice test before any big examination. My method was not singing. They were already in the 9th

73

thru 12th grade. Singing days were over. Their reading comprehension and writing skills were the pits.

Guess what? I survived both private and public schools in Puerto Rico. I got my elementary and secondary teaching licenses. I was ready for the National Guard.

When I told my students at "La Ferran" Public school that I was leaving, they started to cry. They liked my method of teaching. I even paid for their graduation hall because that sector is very poor. I was also in the refreshment committee for the graduating class.

I informed them not to worry. I was going to leave the money with the president of the committee.

Also, I told them that I was going to be present on graduation day. The graduation class gave me a medal and a gigantic postcard signed by all my students. It was a very emotional day…

I was sad but at the same time happy because some of my ex-students were going to join the National Guard and I was going to be their English Instructor once again.

Chapter 15

The Betrayal

There are so many funny stories about Adelin and me. I recall the time that she didn't want to be with me or my brothers. She decided to go alone on her date. It didn't go well.

She left the guy flat and went home. We were waiting for her at the train station, and she never showed up.

We decided to go home and tell our parents what happened. To our surprise, Adelin was fast asleep, and we got the beating of our lives.

Adelin told our parents that we didn't want her to be with us. We told our parents that she wanted to be alone with her so-called boyfriend.

My father kept repeating that if we want to go out, the four of us must stay together. Adelin always had plenty of reasons to leave us. We paid the consequences very high.

Chapter 16

Living With Your Sister and Her Husband

Living with your sister and her husband is never a good idea. No matter how good a relationship you have with your sister, you are invading their life.

Living with your sister is a bad idea. When she is married, she has a completely new life. Your presence in her house will make it uncomfortable for both of you.

Should you live with your sister and her husband?

No, you should never consider living with your sister and her husband. Even if you are a teenager or adult, it is not good to interfere in your sister's life.

When your sister is married, she has a life of her own with her husband and kids. She needs her personal space too. They will have their lovely moments. Everyone has their family time which is different from what they have with their siblings.

You are living in her house will ruin their family time. Moreover, if you are an independent adult, you will have your own life as well. Living with your sister and her husband will affect your life too.

Is it good to live with your sister and her family?

You may have a beautiful bond with your sister, but can you adjust with her husband and kids?

When you think of living with your sister and her husband, you will have to consider a few points. It is not about living with only your sister. You will be sharing the house with your brother-in-law and their kids.

They will have a different lifestyle than yours. There are times when you must adjust. If you fail or they fail to compromise, you will end up in bad arguments. In arguments, you cannot ignore heated moments that will hurt all of you.

There are some cases where kids don't respect their uncles or aunts. In such cases, you can't say anything to kids or your sister.

Moreover, your sister has her personal life, friends, and her husband's side of the family. With you living with them she won't be able to call her friends or family over.

Also, think of how your brother-in-law's family will react to you living with your sister. If you are a teenager, you will be a liability to your sister. You will always get sucked into the family drama of your as well as their life.

Will living with your sister and husband affect your life?

Yes, it will affect your life. As an independent adult, you have your own private space. When you are living with your sister and her family, you won't get to enjoy that private space anymore.

You cannot call your friends, or colleagues over. You cannot throw parties and fun nights. You will always have to adjust to their routine and lifestyle.

It may be a good thing to live with your sister. But living with your sister and her husband is a nightmare you don't want to have. Moreover, her husband may not like a disturbance in their life although he might not express it openly.

Chapter 17

Should I Let My Sister Live with Me?

F amily reunions are great for everyone. But what if you must live with your sister?

No doubt siblings share a special bond and support each other in every situation. Living with your sister isn't always bad. You both can create a lovely space and be each other's company. It is always better than living alone or with some stranger.

However, on some levels living with your sister becomes uncomfortable. Today we live in a world where everyone needs personal space and time. You wouldn't want your sibling to invade your private space all the time.

Confused if you should let your sister live with you? We will help you solve it.

Should I let my sister live with me?

No, you should not let your sister live with you permanently. No matter how much you love your sister, as an adult, you cannot live under the same roof.

Nowadays, everyone wants their private space. You will lose your privacy and personal life if you start living with your sister. Slowly you will realize that both of your lives start to meddle with each other.

Moreover, living together as adults means lots of compromises and arguments. No matter how much you avoid it, you will have lots of arguments with your sister. Eventually, you will ruin your relationship with your sister.

Is living with your sister a good idea?

As an independent adult, living with your sister can become a nightmare.

You will have to adjust your life according to her. You can no longer live freely in your own house.

We all have late-night parties, fun nights and have secret relationships. But with a sister living in your apartment, you cannot enjoy these things.

You cannot bring your friends home, throw a house party, or spend romantic nights with your wife or husband. Also, you will always be sucked into family drama.

To worsen the situation if you are a boy, living with a sister gets trickier. Bringing over your boys for a match or fun night gets uncomfortable for your sister.

Are there any pros of living with your sister?

For some living with a sister is a good thing. People sometimes enjoy spending quality time with their siblings. Such people have a strong bond with their sisters. They share every secret and discuss life problems.

These people don't have any problem with living with their sisters.

Keeping the cons aside, living with your sister cannot be such a bad thing. As siblings, you can build your own lovely space.

In case you are suffering from loneliness, living with your sister can be a good thing for your mental health. You will have your sister as your support system to help you come out of alienation and depression issues.

Moreover, you will be living with someone you know. In case you are new to the city, living with complete strangers is risky.

How do I tell my sister to move out?

If you are uncomfortable living with your sister, ask her politely to move out. You can even help her find a safe and affordable house.

Whether living with your sister is a good or bad idea depends on your personality and lifestyle. Ultimately it is your call, and you should decide after weighing down all the pros and cons.

The idea of living with your parents while at university is not a new one. However, the trend has become more popular in recent years due to the high cost of living and housing. There are both pros and cons to this way of living.

Living with parents can be a great way to save money and avoid the stress of finding accommodation in a new city, but it may also mean that you are not able to live independently.

Some people say that living with your parents can be good for you because it means that you are able to save money on rent, food, bills, etc. This is not always true if you are living with your parents because they want you to be there rather than because it is the best option for you.

Living with your parents may also mean that you do not have the opportunity to make friends or feel independent. You may also feel like an outsider in their home and not know how to contribute in certain areas, such as in decision-making.

Chapter 18

Overreacting

Living with my sister and brother-in-law. Am I overreacting??

So, I'm currently living with my sister and her husband. We are two years apart.

They have two beautiful kids. I always pay my rent on time; work a lot I somewhat keep my distance unless my sister is alone with the kids, I'll hang out with her in the living room.

One night my sister and I had an argument over having some respect while I slept, and kids were running around making noise. My brother-in-law yelled in my face and said just shut the fuck up and go to your room.

I was so hurt because my sister allowed him to talk to me that way. I wouldn't allow my boyfriend or husband to talk to any of my family members in that way.

But my sister allows him to talk to me like that. I am 36, my sister is 38 and her husband is 45.

I'm wrong for it. It's not the first time he has disrespected me like that, and my sister is ok with it. I told her that my 6 yrs. old niece doesn't respect me, and she said you must earn it.

Like wtf?! I am too nice to them, always treat them out for breakfast or dinner and buy whatever the kids need, and I feel so unappreciated. I have been looking to move out in the next few months. Any advice??

Accelerate that move. My guess is he might've been resistant to this set up for this very reason.

A boyfriend is not the equivalent of a husband. Please know that if you try to pull the sister card all the time, you have become a source of tension between them. Same if you hope they will alter how they handle their kids just to suit your preferences. The kids are in their home. You are merely a tenant in the house.

Chapter 19

Meeting Raymond

Adelin was always a very quiet child. She told me so many terrible incidents that happened when she was married....

The begin of her relationship with Raymond Borges. This is how they met.

Adelin had a friend named Lillian. I didn't like Lillian or any of her relatives. She always had this nasty grin that I hated.

Every Saturday, we went to different friends' house. It was like a club. The only one that wasn't married was my sister Adelin. That is when this stupid so-called friend decided to introduce Adelin to a single guy.

I never bothered doing so, because I always believed that she was so beautiful that she will me her future husband on her own.

Well, Lillian pay me no mind. She invited Raymond to one of our gatherings. It was nice meeting everyone like this at different locations. Each couple would bring a special dish.

At our gatherings, we will play dominos, cards etc. My house was the best because I had a pool table and a ping pong table. I also had a bar. That bar was always well packed. There were all kinds of beverages. From simple soda pops to hard liquor.

When it was Lillian's turn, she invited Ray. I didn't like the guy at all. My sister didn't seem too pleased either.

They exchanged phone numbers. Every day they were on the phone for hours. They only met on Saturdays.

What I didn't like about Raymond was that he didn't like chaperons. He also told my sister that they would not go to our Saturday gathering. He wanted to be alone with her.

Well guess what? My sister told my mother that she was old enough to go alone on a date with anyone. My mother was so upset that we had to take her to the hospital.

My father called Raymond and told him what the intention with my sister were. He got furious. He told my dad that they were just dating and that there was no commitment between the two of them.

My father was so upset that he told my sister to stop going out with him. She didn't listen....

Adelin told him that she had a plan. The plan was that if he really loves that they would get married.

They got engaged a couple of months after....

The big question was the wedding date. Raymond told her to start saving because he wasn't going to pay for the wedding. I told my sister that I would help.

My sister had a great job with the Federal Government. She was making three times his salary. He told me that she was supposed to give him her check because they were engaged. Of course, my sister refused.

As the wedding date was approaching, I paid for flowers, photos, and everything necessary. My parents never gave a cent. My mom gave her money to buy the wedding dress.

It was a beautiful wedding on October 1, 1977. The minute they got married he managed her money. She never saw a cent. My sister was a sharp dresser. All that was in the past.

He took her check and disappeared from Monday until Friday. He told her that he was in a business trip. Adelin never told me anything. She was at her apartment crying all the time.

I was married and my ex-husband got alone with my entire family. Grandmother used to come over every Friday to play bingo. We played bingo, dominos, and cards. There was the Bing pong game going and the pool table.

Adelin and Ray were never present. I will tell you why...

Raymond had a mistress. A low life bitch. He used to live with her. That bitch was even present at their wedding. I never told my sister because she never said anything about his disappearance.

After Raymond died, 20 yrs. later, my sister told me every single episode of her life with this jerk.

I was so furious. I always defended my sister, and this happened without my knowledge. My dad knew he had another apartment and my brother Papo. My dad only said that he bought her a nice house in Long Island. That house was very far from us. Adelin was the one that purchased the house, not the idiot.

You know my sister and me were like twins. If she felt, I will feel it....

I used to be sad all the time and I didn't know why.

Now that she is gone, I miss her a lot. She was my only friend....

Chapter 20

Living a Fantasy

The husband, who, for the space of twenty years, has not always been such a wonderful person.

He, Raymond Borges, was living a fantasy. He was a husband and the father of two.

My sister Adelin was really running that household. He didn't deserve a wonderful and caring person like her.

In the meantime, his parents were always looking down on her. His mother, Grace, was always saying that my sister was not the ideal girl for her son.

I was always arguing with Grace or anyone that put down my little sister.

Let me tell you how close we were. I wrote an imaginary story…

Two Sisters

Once upon a time there were two girls who were sisters who did everything together. Sometimes they got into fights.

One time, when they had one of their spats, it was heated! It was the nastiest one they ever had.

Each girl said something that they regret. Of course, I will not tell you what they said. We wouldn't want to embarrass them, would we?

Anyway, the two girls got into a fight because the oldest was telling the younger one what to do. "Stop telling me how to thread the needle!" shouted the younger one named Adelin. "I'm not a baby!"

"Well, I was only trying to help!" yelled Norma, the older one. "Besides, you don't know how to sew half as well as I do!"

So, it went. Norma always firing a comment at Adelin. Adelin always answering back.

This went on until Adelin burst into tears. "Fine! I'm leaving and doing my sewing elsewhere!" Adelin shouted, through tears.

Norma, too shocked to react, watched dumbfounded as Adelin stormed out of the house. "Well good riddance!" Norma called after Adelin, who was already out the door.

The next day, Norma woke up and called for Adelin. "Adelin, come on! It's time to get up!"

She waited for Adelin to reply. When Adelin's voice never called back to her, it suddenly dawned on her that Adelin was not there.

"Well, it doesn't matter that she is gone," Norma murmured to herself, "I'll simply go about my business."

After just a few minutes of trying to do her daily routine, she just couldn't focus. "I can't believe what I said to Adelin!" she cried, "I am so sorry! I must find her and apologize!"

At that same moment, in a grassy field, where Adelin ended up, Adelin was having similar thoughts.

"I wonder what Norma is doing," she said, the words flowing out of her mouth like a waterfall, and she, unable to stop them. "I'm so sorry that we fought. I must go and say sorry!"

So that is what happened. Norma searched the town for Adelin. Adelin hurried home to find Norma.

"I wonder where Adelin is! I have searched everywhere." Norma said, as she felt tears swelling in her eyes, "Maybe she really is mad at me, and never wants to see me again. I guess I'll go home."

Since Adelin was younger, and she seldom went anywhere without her big sister, it took her a little bit more time to get to her house.

While she was wandering, little did she know that a masked man was hiding in the bushes, watching her every move, and mentally taking note of her.

Norma reached home right as Adelin stepped foot on the driveway. "Adelin?" Norma cried out in joy, "Is that you?!"

"Norma?"

"Oh Adelin, I am so sorry! It was plain awful what I said to you! Will you forgive me?"

"Only if you forgive me!" Adelin said, tears streaming down her face.

After the sisters had hugged and exchanged stories, Norma giggled. "You know, you should have seen your face when you saw me," Norma laughed, "You turned pale!"

"Well, you should have seen your face," Adelin said, joining in on the laughter,

"You looked like you'd struck gold!"

"Adelin, I think that we should turn in. It has been a long day."

"You are right," Adelin agreed.

As the girls went inside their house, the masked man cruelly smiled, because his plan had fallen into place.

The sisters didn't even know what was coming...

Adelin woke up in the middle of the night. She expected to wake up in her room, with Norma on the bed across from her on the other side of the room.

That is when she saw all of her and Norma's possessions stretched across the floor.

Instead, she woke up unable to see anything, and heard two gruff voices. "I told you we could do it! The town will never know what hit them."

"I know, I know. But the plan isn't fully complete yet."

The two men went on talking as Adelin felt a hand beside her. "Norma?" she dared to whisper.

"Adelin?" It was Norma!

"Norma where are we? I'm scared."

"Adelin, I hate to say it, but I think we've been kidnapped."

Adelin felt fear flood through her body. Before she was able to question her sister's theory, she felt the automobile stop.

"Adelin, I need you to pretend you are asleep."

"What?!"

"Just do it!"

So as Adelin's blindfold was uncovered, she shut her eyes. She felt herself being picked up by two sturdy hands and put on the grass. Her kidnappers took the blindfold and tied her hands together.

"Pete lets light a fire. I'm cold."

"Okay, but just a small one. We don't want to give away that we're here, and send off a smoke signal."

As Adelin heard the two men's feet shuffling away from her, Adelin opened her eyes and whispered frantically in the dark for her sister.

"Norma, are you here?!"

"Yes. Keep your voice down. Adelin, I think I can get out of this blindfold.

When the man tied it around my hands, he didn't do it very tightly."

As Norma said this, Adelin could barely make out the shape of her sister inside a strange tent.

When she looked around, she realized the men had placed her in a teepee like tent. Norma managed to free herself, and untied Adelin. "Follow my lead."

Adelin whispered in the dark. Adelin decided that it was wise to stay quiet so she let her sister talk. "I can't believe that we got away from those men." Liza said in a very loud voice. Adelin caught on.

"I thought you tied their hands, Jeff!"

"I did!"

"Well, we can't let them get away! They will ruin this whole thing! C'mon!"

Sure enough, the two men went around the tent expecting to find the girls behind the tent.

Norma grabbed Adelin's hand and they ran out of the tent. Norma stopped briefly to grab the keys from the kidnappers' truck so the men could not chase them and catch up by riding in their automobile.

The two girls broke into a run and headed for town. The run seemed like days to Adelin. She was wondering how Norma was doing.

Norma was scared. When the two girls had been kidnapped, she tried to stay calm and did not let her younger sister know that she was petrified.

Then, she had the idea of faking that she and Adelin were behind the tent. She was lucky that she and her sister got away.

Now, clutching the keys of the two kidnappers' car, she finally breathed. She and Adelin were safe and that's all that mattered. "Mr. Cora! Mr. Cora!"

Adelin was shouting.

"What is it?" the police officer said, walking out of a building.

"We've... you see... well we..." Adelin stammered out of breath from the running.

"I'll explain." Norma said, putting a hand on her sister's shoulder. When she was through talking, Mr. Cora stroked his beard thinking. He told the girls that he would send out police officer to search for the kidnappers.

Five days later the girls got a call. "Yes?" Norma called into the phone eagerly, after finding out it was Mr. Cora.

"Norma, we have found the men who kidnapped you and your sister. They confessed to why they kidnapped you.

I'll be over in five minutes to explain.

So, seven minutes later, Officer Cora was sipping the lemonade Adelin had served him.

"Girls, I know you are wondering why you were kidnapped," Mr. Cora began, "The two men confessed, and the reason they kidnapped you is because they wanted to create a distraction.

You see, they were going to leave you two deeper in the woods and while everyone was searching for you two, they would rob the bank."

"But why us?" Adelin questioned.

"Well," Officer Cora continued, "They saw you two going around town yesterday. They thought you two would be perfect for their plan."

Then Norma realized it. The reason they got kidnapped was because of their fight! If they hadn't gotten into their fight, then they wouldn't be running all around town yesterday trying to find each other.

One look from Adelin, and Norma knew that they both had come to the same conclusion.

Well, things weren't that different from then on. Except that the girls never fought again because every time a debate started, they looked at each other and remembered the saga.

Chapter 21

My Number One Fan

My sister Adelin was my number one fan. Every time I wrote something, I would call her and read the story. The following was one of her favorites. I hope you like it as much as she did....

<u>The Oath</u>

People do things differently and quietly in the country. They keep a sort of private council to themselves and never once break that oath.

Opinions are often felt but not spoken. It is just something that is understood. Carmella had always known that she would marry Louis. From the time they played in each other's yards.

She had made up her mind that she was going to marry him. Once a female locks down on an idea, even one the age of seven, then there is little that can change it. Of course, it was not that Louis really had any objections.

Louis went through his usual "I hate girls" phase with the exception of Carmella, whom he considered almost a boy. She fished with him and played ball with him.

She also wandered all over the countryside with him. They were always together. Even if their parents did not understand it, the two of them did.

School came and went, and they grew. They wandered away from each other to others but always came back eventually to who they were.

It was no surprise to anyone when they married after high school.

They live in a very small town and hard times had set in upon it. Yet, they both managed to find a way to work. They saved for the house on the end of the last street that they knew someday would come up for sale.

At the end of five years, they bought the house. The old lady that lived there passed on and her children put it up for sale. Good savings and a good name bought them the house. Life was almost perfect!

When the first baby was stillborn, Carmella grieved and Louis worried but after a while, they tried again.

This time they had a wonderful little boy and a sister followed two years later. Life was once again almost perfect.

Carmella worked, nevertheless she was still a good mother. Louis was growing tired from the constant responsibilities. His eyes wandered and his thoughts strayed, and life was nowhere near almost perfect anymore.

Sometimes, people just need a wake-up call to see what they have. A near fatal wreck from too much drinking almost took Louis' life.

The truth surfaced when the strange woman in his truck was found with him. Carmella kept her opinion to herself and nursed her husband back to health. Louis mended and slowly Carmella withdrew.

Once duty was done and no longer bound, Carmella left, taking the children with her.

Opinions stayed silent but sometimes, life just never is almost perfect. Keep the faith; keep the love alive and keep the dream awake and life has a better chance of being almost perfect.

Louis had to learn that the hard way. When I spoke to him a week ago, he was doing all he could to win back Carmella's love and trust.

Let me tell you that this was based on a true story. Carmella was Adelin's best friend and Louis …. well Louis was her ex-boyfriend….

Chapter 22

The Pub Scene

Adelin helped me write the following story. She was my main fan who criticized everything I wrote. I enjoyed that because I saw how good I was getting as time passed by....

I adjusted my strapless bra before venturing into the club. I always hated strapless bras, I always hated feminine clothing period.

Before you get me wrong, let me introduce myself. My name is Jenny Reyes. I always wanted to be an Angelina or a Crystal, I'd even settle for the name Sarah. But no, I was cursed with my bland, mediocre name Jenny.

Now the reason I hate feminine clothing is another story. Besides the fact that I'm just not like all the other girls in college, even the ones who work alongside me in the library.

I just don't look good in tight jeans and belly shirts. The reason is that I'm fat, plain and simple; I'm an extra, extra, extra-large girl. I know I'm a lot less than attractive, and I know I don't ever really turn heads.

Oh, I turn my head but not in the way I want. I can tell when I walk into a room, people look at me like "Oh my, look at the tub of lard" then nudge and smile at one another.

You'd think I belonged to a circus side show or something the way the people at Old Navy and American Eagle treat me when I come in there to shop.

Can you believe a shoe store once had the audacity to refer me to an online shoe warehouse because my feet were 'just too luscious for the high heel pumps my heart so desired?

Well, if you have then you can empathize with me, and if not then welcome to the world of fat.

On with my resort… I am near the double doors of "The Love Shack," sounds corny I know but it's the only club within 100 square miles of where I live so I take advantage of it.

Being the kind of girl I am, people usually assume I like to stay home and bury myself in books or hide behind a computer screen.

Boy, are they badly mistaken. I spend my spare time in bars, and clubs, hanging out in places just like The Love Shack.

You see, in high school I learned a valuable lesson. All the cheerleaders hated me, all the jocks mocked me.

I was a nobody to everybody that meant anything in that school. When I tried to make friends with girls in my classroom, they would fly away from me.

They would be laughing with one another "can you believe Jenny Jones actually wrote me this letter asking me to be her friend."

They'd wave my large, sloppy handwriting amongst one another like some sort of parade banner. Up and down the hallways giggles would erupt as pretty girls with nice legs and hair turned to point at me and laugh.

Oh, I learned a thing or two back then. Especially that a fat girl like me didn't have a chance with the guys. That is until I discovered a bar one late college night.

My English Professor, Mrs. Cruz. told me one day before an exam that if I'd spend some time unwinding the night before a test it'd do my nerves a world of good.

I asked her for a good place, and she replied, "Why Jenny, a club or even a few drinks at a bar would do the trick." I spent that night in my dorm scouring the local phone book for the nearest bars and dance clubs. That's how I found The Love Shack.

Needless to say, that weekend I found myself in this very place I stand right now. The first time I ever walked through those aluminum, black double doors glinting against the many parking lot headlights.

I just felt like a different person. I nervously took a seat at the bar and ordered what I heard the guy next to me order, a vodka and tonic.

At first taste my whole mouth and throat burned....

After a while, I became accustomed to its strong taste, but little did I know the effect that three of those would have on me.

Before I knew it I had at least four men whirling me around the dance floor. They were damned near fighting over me, that's when I realized these places were different than the outside world.

Men here loved girls like me. A whole lot of fat and a little bit of trashiness found me in a Motel 9 that night with a quite handsome man lying beside me.

True, his breath didn't smell like roses and his lovemaking left a lot to be desired in my opinion but nonetheless I lost my virginity that night.

It wasn't until he dropped me back off at the dorm that I learned the ropes of bar-night dates.

"Will I see you again next week," I asked him in that hopeful, schoolgirl voice with a few bats of my eyelashes for effect.

"Sorry, honey," he replied with a sheepish smile and a scratch of his head. "I'm just a truck-driver in town for the weekend. Next week I'll be making love to my wife I hope."

"Oh," I was about as speechless as I'd ever been, and I knew I was blushing as I stumbled out of his pick-up truck.

"You were a fine young thing in bed though, have to give you that," he tipped his cowboy hat and drove off as I stood there drinking in exhaust fumes and watching the rusty bumper of his truck disappearing into the foggy night.

The following weekend, I decided to play by my own rules. I dressed in some fishnet pantyhose I found on sale at Wal-Mart, a short black miniskirt with a red silk shirt and those black high heels that I did find on the internet.

I painted my lips and my nails in the same shade of crimson. Then, I purposely overdid the eye make-up and teased my hair. I knew I looked like the queen of trash and that's exactly the look I was going for.

You see, I wasn't there for a beauty contest and for respect; I was there simply to have a good time and find me a nice, handsome redneck to jump into bed with.

Again, that night, the men flocked to me. That weekend found me lucky as I spent Friday, Saturday, and Sunday with a red-neck hunk in his truck camper. Boy was he a romantic one, writing me all sorts of love poetry and leaving roses on my pillow for when I woke up.

The sex was incredible; he had the nicest working tongue on any man I've ever met at the bar before. I had planned on seeing him again but learned a few weeks later that he'd been shot and killed during a family feud somewhere in Kentucky. Now, wasn't that just my luck?

But tonight, was going to find me even luckier, I just knew it for two different reasons. For one, a tall, lanky guy in dirty jeans with greasy blond hair was getting close to me.

Now, he might not have been a Playboy, but he sure did have nice teeth and pretty eyes. And those hands, I'd love to feel them work my body over. Now for the second reason, I'd made myself a nice little trip to Sexpot, a sex-toy store a few miles out of town. Tonight, I carried with me some handcuffs, a whip, and a pair blindfold.

"Hello there pretty lady," he said to me in the sexist voice I'd ever heard, and I just knew I'd be putting my special toys to good use tonight with this sexy number.

"Why hello, can I interest you in a night at Motel 9," I asked him as I batted my long, black eyelashes and licked my lips.

"You sure can," he answered me, and I felt myself getting wet as I reached my hand into my bag for reassurance that my toys were still with me.

Now, I know men just want me for my body. I know I'm destined to be a fat ass nobody all my life just because I was blessed with bad genes.

I know I'm forever banished from the 'in crowd.' I know full well I'll never find a man to love me and settle down with me.

I especially know that no man will ever adore on me the way my stepfather adores my mother like she's God's gift to women.

He always did look at me with distaste in his eyes, but he kept his mouth shut about my ugliness to keep my mom happy.

My mom well let's just say she never loved me. No one will ever love a fatso like me, that's why tonight someone must suffer for it.

Too bad pretty boy here had a bulge in his jeans when I scanned the place, otherwise, he might not have been the one to die tonight.

Chapter 23

The Storyteller

You know why I miss my sister so much? We talked for hours about everything. When she was sad, I would call her and read. She told me that I had a pretty voice. She also told me that I should become a storyteller. I just laughed and kept on reading the piece you are going to read.

The Shrine for Lonely Hearts

There was a shrine protected by time, distance, and space. This shrine stood on an island that was only known in dreams, therefore, it was far beyond physical reach.

To some it was known as the Shrine for Lonely Hearts because it was a place where prayers were made for a special wish or love. It had no given idol.

This shrine was built for dreamers to leave their offerings of hope. Anyone who desired something enough and deserved it was then granted entrance into "The Shrine for Lonely Hearts" or so the legend said...

There was a young woman, tender in her years and had a settled life within her small town. She had loving parents and caring siblings.

She was loved by neighbors for her kindness and her art of healing. She was not a beauty on the outside, though not unkind to the sight. She had a few suitors but none that could claim her heart.

As the years passed, she saw her parents age and her brothers and sisters grow. They all got married and became parents themselves.

The suitors around her became fewer as the village was small and eventually, there were none. She was still endeared and loved but her future seemed to be alone.

The years continued to pass, and her parents left this world for a better place. She knew the joy of children from her many nephews and nieces but there was none of her own.

She continued to nurse the sick, be a midwife, and serve her town as best she knew how. Her tender heart and generous nature earned her a special place and gave her much happiness.

Yet, within her, was a hollow emptiness that nothing could seem to fill, and she was lonely until she slept at night.

Thirty years had passed and each night they had met at a bridge. The lovely stone bridge was over a stream of clear cool water that was murmuring and singing over the smooth stones.

The bridge led to a path that wound through a garden filled with flowers of every type, ferns, and whispering willow trees.

They would walk hand in hand in the moonlight and find the bench beside the fountain and there they would sit. He never spoke but she knew what he felt and, each time, as he would lean down to kiss her, she would awaken, losing him to the daylight and only to find him in the night.

He was as young as she when they first met but he aged as she aged. He was still gentle and handsome. A man she had never seen but she felt she knew him and had always known him.

It was always the same place, the same night, and the same walk, only she and he changed with the years.

One day, there came a motive for her to travel to a city away from her quiet town. On the night before the trip, she did not dream of the man and the park but of a shining white shrine on a flourishing island.

She entered the shrine and found only herself there. There were no decorations except a small altar before a beautiful mural of a perfect heart.

She walked to the altar which after all was only a small pool of glistening water that sparkled in the light from an unknown source.

In her right hand, she found she had a large silver coin and not knowing how she knew, she tossed the coin into the pool. It cut the water and then drifted slowly downward and came to rest among a multitude of other identical silver coins.

She knew she had made a wish, and this was the act of it. Then she awakened, disturbed and sad that she had missed her nightly rendezvous with her silent and unknown lover.

The journey to the city by train was boisterous and fast. She wasn't used to none of that. She arrived that night at a station, but no one was there to pick her up from the barrister's office where she had been summoned.

Being confused and uncertain, she saw a small park beside the station and decided to take a walk in the moonlight.

Having lived in a small and safe town all her life, she did not think of any possible danger.

The mature woman walked down the path lined with bushes and willow trees. It twisted and turned, but finally came to a stone bridge.

When she saw the bridge, her heart stopped as if it was the one in her dream. She was afraid to look on the other side.

She was so happy when she looked and saw him standing there. This time he was real and very much alive!

They met in the middle of the bridge, and he took her hand and said nothing. They walked down the path to the bench by the fountain and sat down.

When he leaned down to kiss her, she did not wake up, but instead felt the kiss and it was very real. It was sweeter than anything she had ever imagined.

He stared into her face and said in a warm mellow voice. "I am the barrister that sent for you after spending so many years looking for you.

Since we have been meeting in our dreams all these years and one week ago, I dreamed of a shrine where I made a wish then I knew I would find you.

I have found you now and we must no longer meet in dreams. I love you and neither of us will ever be alone again." Then he kissed her again and this time, it was sealed with a promise.

The end or is it a new beginning? What do you think?

Chapter 24

The Denial

There are so many stories that I didn't get a chance to share with my sister. That is the reason I am writing them in this book because it is dedicated to her....

The first time Robert left me I wasn't devastated. We have been married for over twenty years. Within that period, he was such an angel.

He was always helping around the house. Then suddenly, he made a big change. I guess he was having problems at work. Robert worked so hard for the university that finally he got promoted dean of the English Department.

So therefore, I didn't pay much attention to his changes.

I often heard of men going through those psychologists termed "midlife crisis" around the age of forty. Robert was forty-two and I deemed his affairs a normal stage of life that he'd out-grow eventually. Robert was ten years my senior. I figured sooner or later he'd come to his senses.

I knew Robert loved me more than anything. I knew that once he realized what he was jeopardizing he'd put an end to it.

I can still remember the first time I laid eyes on Robert. The day was warm with just hint of breeze. I remember distinctly how the wind blew through my hair during the walk across campus to the Brooklyn College Library. The sidewalks were littered with kids, books in arms, scurrying to their next class.

Couples walked hand in hand, gazing lovingly at one another while other students stopped to chat with friends.

That year I was a senior in college. I was facing my first crisis. I wanted to change my major from Social Work to Humanities concentration in English.

This didn't look like a pretty sight with my parents. My dad spent an hour lecturing me about the cost of three more years in college.

My mother, of course, had to get her two cents in about when I was ever going to settle down with a "respectable" man.

Finally, I made it through the sidewalk traffic and was rummaging through my backpack outside the library doors when suddenly the door swung open.

Before I knew it, I found myself lying on my back. The contents of my backpack scattered all over the lobby. I must have been momentarily knocked out because a handsome man with black hair and brown eyes stood over me.

"Can you see how many fingers I'm holding up?" he had asked while holding up three fingers on his left hand.

"Yes." I smiled weakly, embarrassed at how silly I must have looked lying there. Three fingers I answered. I'm fine, although I appreciate your concern.

"Well, if you are sure." He seemed to be looking for the right words to say. "Well, if you are okay I'm going to head back to my office." He headed towards Chaucer's Hall, otherwise referred to as the "English Building" by fellow students.

I was moving as quickly as possible, trying to get my stuff together so I could get the hell out of there. I was also hoping he'd take the hint and go away.

I had already humiliated myself; I didn't want to further the execution of my pride. I bent and hurriedly started stuffing things into my book bag.

Strands of hair had fallen out of my ponytail and were sticking to my forehead. I kept puffing air, trying to blow the hair away from my face.

Apparently, the stranger took that as labored breathing and halted on his way out the double doors.

"Hey, are you sure you are, okay?" He began walking back towards me and I silently cursed my own stupidity. "Why don't you let me take you to the student cafeteria for some coffee? We'll talk for a few minutes and if you seem okay after that I'll just go on my merry way."

I was looking into those chocolate-brown eyes and hoping he didn't see my instant attraction to him.

Apparently, he didn't, the only thing on his mind was gathering the rest of my books. I watched him bend to pick up my Physics book and marveled at the view of his ass.

I flinched at my own thoughts, now when did I ever ponder on men's asses, or even think that way in the first place? Here I was, Maria Rivera, a bookworm, checking out this man I didn't even know.

I was sure he must be a professor, although I'd never had him for a class personally. Still, I felt revolted at the thoughts that were slowly etching their way into my silly head.

Once seated in the cafeteria and happily slurping on a Mocha Cappuccino, I allowed myself to stare dreamily into his eyes and be carried away with his life story.

He was unhappily married to an older lady who adored him in a motherly way. I couldn't understand why that shocked him, considering his looks, and I was sure any woman in her right mind would dote on him, and rightfully so.

Why he decided to pour his heart out to me I still do not know, but I am glad. On that very day, Robert Torres became my first real boyfriend.

I usually leave out the fact that on that very day I became a married man's mistress for the first time, but right now I'm feeling more open than usual.

Robert was also the first man I ever slept with. It happened on the night of our first month anniversary. Robert and I had made a habit of having cappuccino in the student's cafeteria every evening.

I always brought my literature books and I'd spread them open to some random pages, so it'd look as if Robert was tutoring me.

We had coffee while Robert told me about his separated wife. It was sad listening to the stories on how his wife recently cheated on him, and how they'd tried but could never conceive.

Robert wanted to be a father and she never bothered to go for medical assistance. He also added, a bit jokily, that she had no real sex drive while his was still out of this world.

One thing led to another and before I knew it, I offered to let Robert take me out for a romantic night around town.

We began at The Movies, where we watched some cheesy action flick. I probably shouldn't even say we watched it, because I bet, we spent over half of the two hours playing tongue tag.

Afterwards we had banana splits from Baskin Robbins. Robert insisted on watching the sunset at the lake to top off an "absolutely enchanting" evening.

Now, I hadn't been in the dating business very long, but I sure hadn't felt that a make-out session and banana splits were all that enchanting.

The first time we made love happened while we were waiting for the sun to set. I felt kind of silly, just sitting there with Robert, gazing out the windshield into the cloudy sky.

I realized that the sun had obviously already set because it was quickly becoming dark.

Robert reached over and gently pulled my face to his own. Over the past few weeks, I'd gotten used to Robert's romantic kisses.

We often stole a peck or two while riding the elevator in the Chaucer building, but the way Robert was kissing me that night was something I'd never experienced.

One thing led to another, and I found myself lying in the back seat, with Robert thrusting into me with what seemed like all his might.

Two weeks later, while watching yet another sunset, Robert asked me to close my eyes. I absolutely wasn't expecting it, but my heart jumped for joy when I felt him slip that engagement ring on my finger!

I cried and cried until my nose began to bleed, then I cried some more because the sight of blood always freaks me out.

All that time Robert held my hand. He stated that we were going to have a wonderful life together. Things were wonderful, until that first affair.

Afterwards, Robert pledged he would never do it again, everything seemed wonderful again. He had gotten down on his hands and knees and cried and begged me to forgive him; his actions gave the promise that things were going to improve between us.

For a few years they did improve. Everything was hunky dory, even in the bedroom!

Then, Robert abruptly started coming home later than usual. When questioned about it, he just told me he was having a very busy semester; some students needed extra tutoring in English Literature.

At first, I bought his stories, until one day I decided to do some detective work. Robert called me from his office. He said that he'd be home a few hours later than usual. I decided to go out and investigate. I wanted to know if he was telling the truth.

I squeezed my red focus into a parking spot where I was nestled behind a double cab pick-up and two other red cars. I was positive that Robert would never notice me sitting there.

He thought I'd never spied on him. I never did so why would he expect it to happen out of the blue?

I strummed my fingers nervously against the steering wheel while soaking in the nostalgic scenery.

Sure enough, ten minutes later, at five o'clock, the end of Robert's workday, I saw him rushing towards the parking lot. He jumped into his car. He was really in a hurry and high-tailed out of there. I gave him ten seconds and then I eased out onto the highway and followed him.

I made sure I kept my distance by leaving two cars behind. About five minutes into the trip. I saw him take a right turn, I quickly changed direction my car into the right lane and continued to pursue him.

I noticed vaguely that we'd entered a rather wealthy neighborhood. Condo's and huge two- story houses lined the streets on both sides.

A sign on the side of the road read "Regency Estates," and I must admit I was impressed with the size of the lawns.

Night was falling and I realized if I didn't pay attention, I'd totally lose Robert. I sped up a bit and up ahead I spotted him pulling into a Victorian style home.

I gave him about five minutes, and then eased my car onto the parking area on the street opposite the house. He was escorted into the house.

My eyes took in the wooden Victorian with its wrap around porch and its huge, black banister balcony.

The grounds were elegantly tended if I must say so myself. I figured the woman who lived there must either have a wealthy husband, or she'd fallen into some money somewhere down the line.

What kind of career woman would find the time to go gallivanting around with a married man?

I tried my best to keep my mind occupied while waiting for Robert to come out. I listened to the radio, counted the trees on the street, and even risked a small nap.

Despite my efforts I couldn't get the thought out of my head that at this very moment, about twenty yards away, some strange woman lied in her bed making love with my husband.

I was contemplating on creating a nice appearance when suddenly the front door opened and I could see two figures, silhouetted in shadow, standing on the porch.

The woman wrapped her dirty man-stealing hands around my husband's neck. She pulled him to her for a long embrace. This was followed by a five-minute kiss and then another five-minute conversation before Robert finally maneuvered his way across the Martha-Stewart-like yard.

His hair was messy, and I knew instantly that my instincts were correct. I have to say it was more common sense than anything. Any idiot could put two and two together; even a child could sum those events up to one cheating husband and one rich mistress.

At first, I never confronted Robert; I let this go just to see how long he would on without confessing.

In my heart I knew that Robert loved me. I was so sure that he was only impressed with Ms. Cute Lawn's wealth and community status. I mean, it must be a huge ego stroke to know that a rich woman desired you. One year passed and Robert still never confessed.

One day during dinner I was rehearsing in my head exactly how I was going to approach this subject when Robert muttered, "I'm getting a divorce."

Little explosives shot off in my head. Still, I didn't say anything, I feared I must have heard wrong. Robert and I had been married for twenty-five years.

I had given up college and my career of writing so that I could keep his house, cook his dinner, and wash his clothes.

I have given up my dream on having a child because he was barren and didn't wish to adopt a child. I'd sacrificed the very core of myself, and my morality, to keep this man next to me!

Why would he want to leave me? Why would any man want to leave a woman who would let him have his cake and eat it too?

"I simply don't love you anymore, Maria. That is plain and simple. We've just grown apart in the last three years.

At first, I thought it was a mid-life crisis but now I know it's not. "Robert threw his spoon onto his plate and wiped his mouth with a napkin before standing.

So, there was my answer. Robert didn't love me anymore. After I had devoted twenty-five years of my life to this man, watched him cheat on me night after night he is telling me that he is getting a divorce.

I sacrificed everything that had ever been important to me, and Robert still didn't care...

"This is hard to say, Maria." I couldn't believe there was more still. "I'm not sure if I ever did love you. Come to think of it, I think I was just mad with infatuation.

I mean, a young college girl, in love with me. We just sort of grew on each other. Now I realize it just wasn't meant to be."

That was that, not even an apology. Robert didn't apologize! But I know he loves me; I know he does.

I could see it in the way he glanced at me the last time he was home. The night after he'd packed all his bags, he was to be gentle.

I can tell he loves me because he gave me the house, the property and everything in it. We didn't even have to settle in court. I know Robert loves me...he just didn't realize it yet.

Robert was simply in a state of denial; therefore, I'd wait for him to realize the mistake he had made.

When Robert left, I continued to keep a look-out on him. I keep a schedule every semester of all his classes.

I've even managed to clean a key to his office on campus. Sometimes late at night I let myself into the back door of the building and glide gracefully into his office. He has an old green, plaid couch that's fringed around the arms.

It's been there ever since I was a student, and it brings back bittersweet memories of our early love-making sessions. I often put some music on from his classical collection, make me a cup of coffee on his coffee maker and relax on that couch. I know this might sound crazy, but that couch smells just like him.

I often drive by where he lives now. I must confess he did well with his fourth wife, she looks much better than the one he left me for.

This new one is a little blonde, she looks to be no older than 25. They live in a beautiful stucco house with an indoor pool. His new woman obviously loves candles.

I know that bit of information first-hand because I monitor their where-about closely.

Just last winter they spent two weeks in a romantic cabin they rented in the mountains. It was in those two weeks I found an entry through the basement window without setting off the burglar alarm.

I spent two weeks in Robert's new home, getting to know his surroundings. I ate the food from the fridge and even used the fancy China that carefully decorated the kitchen hutch.

I slept in their bed and pretended I was Robert's new wife. I used her fancy bubble bath, put on her designer make-up, wore her victories Secret's thongs to bed and even masturbated using the tiny vibrator I found in the night-stand drawer.

Before I left the next day, I brushed my teeth with her new toothbrush and I stuffed some of their underwear into my purse, then quickly tidied up before leaving. I must admit that it felt like quite the vacation, yet it didn't cost me a thing.

Tonight, I waited nervously for Robert to return home from work, just like I always do. I make his dinner, I set his place at the table, and I often fix his favorite meals.

He left almost a whole closet full of his clothes and once a week I wash them, press them, and hang them neatly in his closet the way he always liked. I just want him to be happy.

Tonight, is our thirtieth anniversary and I've made his favorite meal of chicken with broccoli and cheese casserole. One thing Robert never forgets to do is comment on my cooking.

It's been ten years since he left me, but that doesn't make me believe in the power of love any less. What is it the great philosophers say, something about true love lasting for eternity.

Well, that's me and Robert for sure. I love him the same as I did the_day I married him, and I know he still loves me even though he's in a state or denials.

There are just some things a woman can tell by intuition alone, and if there's nothing else, I can be sure of in the world I can tell you that my husband does still love me.

So here I sit, waiting for Robert to return. He was supposed to be here already, I had dinner made an hour ago and now it's getting cold. He always hates it when his dinner is cold. I can't imagine what's keeping him. In my heart I always knew he'd come back, and I knew it'd be on our thirtieth anniversary.

That's what happens when one is on denial......

Chapter 25

I know that Adelin would have love this story...

The Magic Town

Rexville was a tiny community, but it had a reputation for being a great place to escape the rigors of city life.

Some say that the place has magic. One can get away to the "great outdoors" and be close to mother nature. It seemed to be the perfect place for Rachel and Bob to go to try and piece back the remnants of their failing marriage.

It was Rachel's idea when she saw the brochure in the beauty shop that another customer had forgotten. The scenery looked stunning with a small but unbelievably clear lake, fed by the melting water of the nearby mountains.

Acres and acres of tall pine and evergreen lined the shores of the lake with widely paced quaint cabins nestled in a clearing here and there. It was perfect!

When she first suggested it to Bob, he did not seem receptive to the idea at all. He objected that it was too far. Secondly, that it was too expensive for their strained budget. The thirdly was silent but they both knew it was there. Why should they go there and spend three days either fighting or in total cold silence?

However, Rachel kept working on him and he finally agreed just to shut her up about it. She called and made the reservations for the cabin, the rental car and organized everything before they left. All Bob had to do was to get ready and then drive.

The drive across two states was done mostly in their habitual silence but Rachel kept herself from showing any anxiety by either reading or sleeping when she was not driving.

She knew that the hours of silence away from his refuge of work and television gave Bob time to think that she knew was very necessary.

After several hours, he was tired of the fading in and out of the radio, same CD's repeatedly and so he began to talk.

The conversation stayed light and proceeded to continue into their meals as they drew closer to Rexville. Rachel was growing more hopeful by the mile and by the minute.

By the time they reached the cabin late that night, she was very encouraged. She said nothing when Bob mumbled a weary good night and promptly went to sleep.

She took hope in the knowledge that they still had two whole days of togetherness ahead of them.

The days seemed to pass quickly beginning the next morning as they rented a small bass boat and went out onto the placid lake to do some fishing. She did not care for fishing, but she knew that Bob loved it.

They spent three fish-less hours on the lake, but Bob seemed to have enjoyed himself as he was more than willing to go on a long walk up the Nature trail with her in the afternoon.

She thrived in the awing majesty of the wooded area and the serene quiet of the walk. Bob also seemed to be pleased with the beauty around him.

They returned to the cabin for a warm meal that Rachel cooked, and Bob ate with a starving, healthy hunger.

She showed her delight when he offered to help with the cleanup. "Yep," she thought to herself, "things are definitely looking up!"

Matters improved even more when he reached for her in bed, and they made quiet but contenting love for the first time in many months. Her plans were working wonderfully.

The next day seemed to be a flawless copy of the first until they sat down for dinner. They heard the wind begin to howl like a banshee.

It seemed to have come from out of nowhere and soon, the lashing rain and booming thunder followed as a mountain storm awakened in the night sky and dumped its wrath upon the tiny lake and even smaller cabin.

The power failed so they lit the kerosene lamps and moved closer to the fire burning brightly in the fireplace.

There on an Indian rug in front of the hearth, they left quiet love behind and took each other to heights to equal the rage of the mad storm outside.

Just at the end, everything suddenly went quiet. The rain stopped, the thunder ceased, and the wind went eerily silent. They both stopped in surprise and listened to the sound of nothing!

Without knowing why, Bob was overwhelmed with an intense sense of fear. He never said a word but quickly rolled his naked wife up in the rug, grabbed his jeans, lifted her, and made an inexplicably quick dash for the door.

She lay silent in his arms, terrified by the unmasked fear on his face. He flung himself through the front door and leaped like an Olympic jumper from the front porch.

At that very moment, a huge- jagged streak of lightning sliced the sky and its sizzling wicked end found a mark on top of a very tall pine that stood at the far western corner of cabin.

The lightning split the tree as neatly as a dagger through flesh and the burning tree groaned, swayed, and then collapsed onto the top of the cabin.

The roof caved and the cabin soon was a shambles of burning pine, varnished logs, and other contents inside, everything but the two humans that had been there just moments before.

The wind began to moan and rise again. The rain fell again but not as hard. The rumbling thunder sounded but with a distinct distance to its sound. The storm was passing.

Unbelieving, Rachel turned and stared in astonishment at the face of her husband. "How did you know?" she whispered. He stared down at her, and his eyes told her his thoughts.

He was thinking of how close he had come to losing her and knew that nothing was worth that. He pulled her close to him as he returned his gaze to the burning cabin and said softly "My grandfather always told me to be cautious when an angry wind suddenly goes quiet it is a warning of danger! My dear wife, I think this proves he was right."

Rachel only leaned closer to her husband, sheltering in his strength and quietly nodded her head in agreement.

Rachel and Bob were rescued by the fire department. They were supplied with clothing and food. Nearby neighbors escorted them to their cabin.

The following day, Rachel and Bob decided to return home. As they drove, there was a feeling of love in the air. Rexville was really a magic town. Their marriage was saved.

THE END

Chapter 26

Serious Situation

Adelin always told me that I had such a vivid imagination.

This is a serious situation that can happen to anyone. Police Officer John Anderson of the 5th Pct, in New York City, is the narrator of this tale. He is trying to write a statement about an incident that occurred in his precinct. ......

Keep in mind that this story is nonfiction, however, I changed the names to protect the innocents.

Sometimes it is critical when we become angry, and that anger turns into mobilized actions designated to eliminate crime and disorder problems that terrorize the safety of any community...

When news of the terrorist attacks reached me, I was working on the piece that follows. It is the story of a single act of aggression inflicted by a police officer on the body of a citizen.

In the day, as the series of act of violence became apparent, it seemed a treat to concentrate on arranging words on a page.

To write a report on this incident, I really had a hard time. I even lost my thoughts.

Many have observed the events of September 11th, 2001, in their own way. It has changed everything. Perhaps it would be more accurate to say that they disclosed the underlying terms of existence as a survivor of violence once observed.

Two weeks have now passed. New York City remains covered with ashes. The aftershock continues to unsettle our lives.

Thousands of tragic individuals narrate experiences and their sufferings. They spoke in detail about their tragic. The testimonies were endless. It was hard for any of them to deal with so much grief.

During much confusion, this much is clear: violence is prepared in the domain of words before it is inscribed on the bodies of human beings.

Consider what had to happen in the semantic realm for those who planned and executed mass murder on September 11th to be capable of such acts.

Consider our national efforts to come to terms with what happened on the 11th: the fates of whole populations now turn on the choices we make between words, on the metaphors we adopt, on the stories we tell.

As The New York Times resumes publication, we rededicate ourselves to the work on resisting violence wherever we encounter it, and in whatever form, by using language responsibly to call things by their true names.

In that spirit, we offer the following report:

One in an ongoing series on police violence in public housing located on the Delancey section of New York City sometimes called by some "Alphabet City".

On the morning of Thursday, September 6th, Johnny Brown went to buy some cigarettes, a 45-year-old resident of New York City.

Brown was visiting a friend who lives in 5419 Avenue C, in housing projects. He descended by way of the stairs because the elevators, as is often the case, were not working.

The open-air lobbies of the "Delancey building," as residents refer to are the setting for an active drug marketplace. It is also the scene of many other activities. There were many residents coming and going throughout the day.

One can see children with brightly colored knapsacks heading out to school in the morning and returning in the afternoon. There were friends enjoying each other's company in convivial public space.

Even when stepping out for just a few minutes, Brown makes a point of taking his wallet containing identification, because he has been stopped by police who threatened to charge him with criminal trespass.

He also carries a letter signed by his friend which states that he is on the development for the purpose of visiting her.

Brown bought some cigarettes three for a dollar from one of the men in the building then chatted with friends.

As Brown was talking to his friends, the police appeared out of nowhere. There were five unmarked cars and a paddy wagon. They were looking for drug dealers. The dealers fled upstairs. The community members in the vicinity began to disperse.

When Brown saw the police, he returned to the lobby… He remembered very clearly that he walked away. He didn't run. He walked at a normal pace. His only intention was to pass through the lobby, out the other side to go to the store.

"I got halfway past the mailboxes," he recalled, "and that's the last thing I remember. I woke up spitting teeth."

According to witnesses, a plainclothes police officer ran up behind Brown and hit him with full force in the back.

It was with something that resembled a football block. The impact slammed him face first to the ground and sent his body skidding forward some fifteen feet.

"It was," a witness said of the sound, "like an egg hitting the ground and smashing." Brown was blind-sided. He had no warning that the blow was coming. The officer said nothing prior to striking him. "He didn't say, 'I'm an officer.' He didn't say, 'Stop!' He didn't say anything."

Witnesses said that the officer's name is Thomas Di Angelo. Everyone knows Di Angelo because he is a corrupted and enjoys abusing his power as a police officer.

Brown passed out briefly. He lay face down on the concrete. His nose was broken. His two top front teeth were knocked out and driven through his upper lip.

"I sat up on the ground, trying to compose myself. Another plainclothes police officer said, 'Get your black ass up.

There isn't anything wrong with you. Get your black ass up.' I rolled over and got on my knees. As I was getting up, he grabbed my arm and slammed me up against the wall."

This police officer took him to the paddy wagon where they were collecting dozens of people they had arrested. As far as Brown knows, he was the only one they roughed up.

He was bleeding profusely. He overheard the sergeant at the door of the paddy wagon say, "Get him out of here." They took him to the paramedics. The paramedic who treated him was very nice.

He took him outside to find his two front teeth in the hope that they could be restored. Because he had been unconscious, the paramedic insisted that Brown be taken to the hospital to be examined and called an ambulance.

The ambulance took him to Bellevue Hospital. He was accompanied by two uniformed officers. "They were really nice," stated Brown. They said they couldn't understand why Police Officer Di Angelo did that to me."

After he was examined at Bellevue, he was taken to the police station. When he entered the station, he heard "some smart remarks like 'You won't try to run from the police no more, will you?'" But he also observed a good deal of uneasiness about his condition. "There were a lot of mixed emotions down at that police station."

He saw the officer who slammed him to the ground. "I asked him, 'Why did you do that to me?' He didn't say anything. He just walked off."

While waiting to be booked, Brown overheard discussion among the police about whether they should give him another charge resisting arrest or selling drugs.

He also heard an exchange in which "they were trying to get someone other than the one that assaulted me to sign the police report." He is not sure what the outcome was. At the end, he was charged with criminal trespass and solicitation of unlawful business.

He was taken to Central Booking at One Police Plaza where he spent the night. In pain from his injuries, he was unable to sleep. He was released on his own recognition on Friday morning and returned to Delancy's Housing Projects.

"Out of my forty-something years, this has never happened to me," Brown observed. "They want to categorize and put everybody in the same boat."

In telling his story, he took pains not to do the same with respect to the police. He didn't to put them all in the same boat. "All police are not bad."

He recalled the solicitude of the two officers who took him to the hospital and the comments of others who were offended by what was done to him.

"Me myself, I don't bother anybody. I treat the police with the utmost respect. If they ask me a question, I answer them. If they tell me to go over there, I go over there. If they tell me to sit down, I sit down. But Police Officer Di Angelo assaulted me to the fullest and thought nothing of it."

Police Officer Anderson thought about the incident. He sees these cases day in and day out. Brown vs. Di Angelo case was treated fairly.

Police Officer Thomas Di Angelo was terminated from the police force. He was sentenced to a five-year sentence for assaulting a citizen. He had other cases pending; therefore, he lost his police pension.

Chapter 27

No Backup

Adelin told me once that listening to my stories was better than any soap operas...

I am retired Detective Michael Mc Donald and the story you are about to read is true. As you read you will be more knowledgeable of the work of a police officer.

During the first several years that I worked as a police officer, I was assigned to the 25 Precinct. That precinct is in Spanish Harlem, in New York City.

My partner was Police Officer Raymond Martinez. We learned to handle many types of calls by ourselves just because there were many times a back-up was not available. Sometimes your back-up was twenty or thirty miles away.

It would be nice to think that the public, the people you are trying to help, would come to your aid, but you quickly learn that all too often they won't lift a hand to help.

There are people out there who will go out of their way to help an officer, but they seem to be few and far between.

It appears that a lot of people feel that officers are paid to take the risks and they aren't paid to get hurt trying to assist the Police.

This may be true, but the officer sees it as just another example of how the public doesn't care about any law enforcement. The wall between the officer and the people he is paid to protect becomes bigger.

One evening, I received a disturbance call from 96 Street and 5th Avenue. The neighbors called and said it sounded like a fight was going on next door. There were about twenty duplex units in this complex.

It was early evening and when I arrived, and I found about half the residents outside in their yards watching what was going on. Police Officer Martinez was busy at the precinct, so I proceeded on my own. I thought that I would go and investigate. It was just a disturbance call....

I could hear shouting coming from the unit I had been sent to. I approached the apartment knowing that my back-up would not arrive for at least ten minutes, due to this location at the time of the call.

The door flew open as I got about twenty feet from it. A man in his early twenties, about my size, came out. He walked as if he was going to just go by me. I told him that I wanted to talk to him.

He said something to the effect that he didn't want to talk to me. He was still about five feet from me when a girl came out of the apartment.

She was crying and bleeding from the nose and mouth. She pointed at the man and stated that he had beaten her up and busted up her apartment.

The man was even with me by this time and still walking. I held out my hand to stop him and told him I wanted to talk to him.

He pushed me and started running. He headed straight toward a group of about ten neighbors who were out in the street watching the show.

They parted like the Red Sea as he got to them. They were shouting for me to get him, but that was as much support as they were willing to give me.

I caught him in the middle of the street and told him he was under arrest. He took a swing at me, and we struggled for a minute or so. He was trying to get away and I was trying to get his arms behind him.

I lost my grip, and he took off running again. I ran him down this time in the front yard of the duplex across the street, again people were all around us, but they acted like this was all a game.

I heard a lot of laughing and cheering. We struggled again. After a few minutes, he broke free and ran from me.

I was angry by this time and tired of playing around. I caught him as he was about to go around the corner of the building, but this time instead of grabbing him I did a flying tackle on him from behind.

There was a large rose bush in front of us and he landed in the middle of it with me on top of him. I managed to knock the fight out of him. I handcuffed him while he lay there. I wasn't going to give him a chance to run again.

Both of us had blood on our faces and arms from the thorn pricks. As we walked toward the patrol car the people just laughed. They were in a very festive mood.

Some of them were clapping and cheering. They may not have cheered so loud if they had known what I thought of all the help they had given me.

My back-up arrived as I was putting my prisoner in the back of my patrol car. Even though everything was over, it surely was good to see another cop.

My sister and I were special ed. Teachers. We sometimes used to talk about cases that were so sad…. This story is true; however, the names were changed to protect the innocents.

Chapter 28

Wendy

Sometimes I think I was molested, others I'm not sure…

At 60, Wendy recovered memories of being abused by her father. She tells her story for the first time

Wendy's home is filled with mementos, collage of photographs, a portrait of her old dog. Her wedding photos and her children.

There are wedding anniversary photos of her parents' 25 anniversary, 50 anniversary and 65 anniversaries. They have been carefully celebrated…

From her bedroom window, she can see the church where she and her husband married. She can even recite every moment of the day. There is a reason for this careful collection. "My memory," she says, "is a matter of some discussion."

In precise tones, Wendy, 60, explains how she came to be part of being a lonely old lady household. This is the first time she has talked to her sister about her story.

For years, she was known only as the lonely sibling.

"When I was about 8, I accused my biological father of sexually molesting me," Wendy says, sitting in the living room of her peaceful split-level home. My mother was either ignoring me and sister. She was always in her own world.

Her parents' marriage seems to be perfect, however, it was far from perfect.

Wendy had flashbacks from her childhood. Too many incidents…

By then eight, she is playing with her crayons. Her dark, curly hair is held back by a pink ribbon, and her smile. She is missing a front tooth.

She remembers that behind her are shelves of heavy textbooks. She looks into mirror occasionally. She articulates for something that a small child would have said. It is only the words that are shocking: a small girl describing how her father has sexually abused her. No one heard those words.

"At that point, since she didn't have any family members to step in and take care of her and her siblings, she stayed quiet.

What she is trying to remember was why her mother left her alone so many times. Her mom will take her sister and her brothers. She was left with that monster of a father.

Over the decades, Wendy forgot what happened...

As time went by, she couldn't remember any more why she didn't see her father trying to touch her. She started seeing her two brothers abusing her.

She recalls one day. She woke up and found herself naked. Her two brothers on top of her. They were putting bobbing pins into her vagina. She was in pain.

She blocked everything from her childhood. Her father and two brothers did harm her.

In school she was very quiet. She didn't tell her teacher or any of her friends. What she remembers the most was that her sister was always protecting her from danger. Little did her sister know was that the enemy and danger was in the house, not outside.

Wendy never told her sister because she was a child herself. She started doing bad in school. She was left back. Her mother didn't do a thing.

One time her father was afraid because Wendy didn't get her period. She was taken to the doctor. Wendy was confused because the doctor asked her if she had a boyfriend. She told her doctor that she wanted to get married as a virgin.

Wendy finished high school and got a great job....

Her parents never praised her or her sister. The boys were the ones that got all the glory even when they did bad in school.

By the age of 26, Wendy met the love of her life. That is what she thought...

At first, he was the perfect gentleman. Took her out and he told her that he would show her the world. She had no idea that this guy was worse than her father.

They did get married after a year or so after their engagement. It was a beautiful wedding.

Wendy paid for everything of course. She had some help from her sister. Her father or mother paid for nothing.

Wendy wanted children because she was getting close to her 30th birthday. Her husband said that they must wait at least five years.

She put her foot down and told him to clean his act.

The jerk was never home. He used to come home and get her paycheck. He would disappear for the next five days. Came to the house with dirty clothes and that was it.

Let me tell you about the jerk....

By the way, his name is Robert. He works at a bank as a clerk. Making little money. The jerk had a mistress. They had a love nest in the Bronx.

Wendy at this point already had a house Upstate New York. Guess what? The jerk purchased the house without even telling her. He manipulated her from the beginning of their relationship.

She just wanted to get married and get the hell out of that house of horror. Her sister was already married. She had no one to talk to in the house.

Robert knew that this sweet innocent individual was going to be easy prey. He wasn't in love with her.

Every time they had sex, she was either drugged or drunk. He did lots of damage not only physically, but also verbally.

Wendy kept quiet. She was so happy with her two kids that she didn't take care of her appearance. His family always praised him on how great he looked.

Robert got worse as years went by. He knew Wendy wasn't going to tell her family.

Adela's sister was noticing that things were not right...

Noriada, Wendy's sister, started investigating the jerk. She found nothing.

One day she got a call from a jerk. He told her that her sister was in the hospital. Noriada found that strange. Her sister was always very healthy.

Noriada told her supervisor that she had to help her sister. She was granted two months leave.

When Noriada reached her sister's house, she found Robert very relaxed watching TV. The kids were happy to see their auntie.

Noriada took the kids to the mall, and they had dinner there. When they returned to the house, they found Robert's sister getting out of the car with her family.

Robert's sister told Noriada that she was coming to stay in the house and take care of the boys.

Noriada told her to get back in the car and go home. She also told her that her sister was coming home the following day and that she was going to be their caretaker...

Chapter 29

A Happy Ending

There are so many stories that I shared with my sister. As I said before, she named me her storyteller...

"Honey, I'm home," he called as he shut the front door behind him.

He set his briefcase down in the foyer and caught a glimpse of himself in the mirror that hung in the living room. He thought he didn't look bad for a middle-aged man.

The dark curly hair had thinned and grayed a little at the temples. The brown eyes were still full of life and sensuality. There were some wrinkles, but he still looked tall, handsome, and authoritative in his police uniform, attractive enough that many women looked at him and smiled at the office or other public places.

There was no reply from his wife and his mind went back to the times when she met him at the door with a smile and a kiss and sweet, concerned conversation about his day.

He felt his face redden and the blood rush to his loins as he thought about the time she greeted him, wearing nothing but her apron and whispered, "Dinner is served."

He remembered how the scent of her perfume enticed him and the beauty of her full breasts beckoned him to touch and taste. He had pushed the centerpiece of flowers and the tablecloth away and they made passionate love on the bare wood of the dining room table.

NORMA IRIS PAGAN MORALES

It had been so long since he had seen the flame of desire burning in her deep green eyes. There were nights his body ached to hold her, to ravish her once again with the heat of his passion just as he had done so many times in the memories of their past that played over and over in his mind.

Memories of her smooth, pale skin, the scent of her long auburn hair, the fire of her kisses tormented him like sensual movies that would never be more than fantasies. Reveries of firelight, candlelight and moonlight, the times, and places they consumed each other with hot desire.

He ached to feel the love in her touch once more, but she no longer desired him and at best made no pretense of anything more than a "Married" friendship, at worst an open war or troubled truce.

He didn't understand why, he was the same man she had married, still devoted to her. Was she having an affair or had he simply failed as a husband?

He found her in the kitchen, this time fully clothed and taking a chicken casserole out of the oven. There was no pleasant greeting or kiss and tonight Cathy got down to business immediately.

"Ray please don't think just because it's what you want makes it what I want. I told you before this is not where I want to live, and you just ignored my wishes. I called the realtor today and he'll be here tomorrow night to list this house and I don't want any more arguments of excuses about staying here."

There was a time he might have asserted his masculinity and his rights, but that time was long gone and now he just wanted peace at almost any price.

"That's fine" he curtly replied.

He was ready to sell the house; the view of the bay meant little to him anymore now that they no longer shared it at dawn or at sunset.

Maybe when the house sold, he would just give Cathy whatever she wanted and quietly disappear. He had a lucrative career and could afford to give her everything and still make a life for himself.

Bobby was almost out of high school; he had raised a sensible and intelligent son, whom he felt would be able to make it just fine without him there every day. They could still spend time together, doing man things.

Maybe there was life after divorce as many of his friends could attest to, but divorce, until now, had never been an option he allowed to enter his mind or plans.

When he took marriage vows before God, he meant them and had done all he could to preserve his marriage and the sacredness of those vows. Now there was never a day that passed that the solution of divorce didn't travel though his thoughts.

Freedom was not what he had wanted but it was beginning to sound better with time and with each rejection she inflicted on him. She was a good person, a giving woman, just no longer good or giving to him.

It seemed an impossibility to touch her heart anymore, not with the expensive gifts of jewelry, the nights out, the tender love poetry he wrote for her. Nothing mattered anymore and he felt like a man drifting in the ocean on a deflating air raft. He was growing tired of begging for her love.

It was time to just let go of all the years, the plans to be together forever. Though he knew in his heart he would love her for the rest of his life, they couldn't spend those years together making each other miserable.

It would be Valentine's Day again in a few days, what should he give her, some emerald earrings to match her eyes, or a divorce? He sighed at the thought that the divorce would make her happier.

"Cathy, I'm going to the store for coffee," he called out over his shoulder as he closed the back door behind him.

There was no reply, and he knew she was glad to have her solitude.

He'd grab a cup of coffee at the convenience store and then ride around aimlessly for an hour or two. Eat microwave-warmed casserole when he got home and hopefully by that time he could go to sleep.

Another day of being alone in a world full of people was the only thing that came to mind.

The convenience store was close by, and the clerks knew him by name. Gloria, a perky, petite, dark complexion Hispanic and a single mom was behind the counter and as soon as she saw him in the parking lot she put on a fresh pot of coffee and a big smile.

They exchanged pleasantries; talked about his son, her two daughters as he waited for the fresh coffee to brew. All the ladies at the convenience store and the hamburger places seemed to adore him, with his good looks and polite manners. He could have gone out with some of them....or done more, even though they knew he wore a wedding ring, but he never allowed the conversation to go in that direction.

He knew he dared not because he was so lonely, and an affair might fill some of the emptiness. If his marriage was going to dissolve, he was determined it would not be because he had an affair.

The night was cold, and he could see the steam billowing out of the heat units of homes and business as he rode around in the Lumina.

The radio was on as usual, turned to the oldies station and tears filled his eyes when some of the love songs brought back memories of young love and stolen touches in the back seat of his car.

He had dated other girls but the moment he met Cathy he knew she was the one. They could barely manage to keep their hands off each other, even in public.

Right after she graduated, two years after him, they married, and it seemed their happiness would never end. He knew he hadn't been perfect, but he couldn't understand what he had done to lose her love.

As he pulled out on the green light into a busy intersection when without warning....BAM!!!

A loud crashing noise and the shattering of glass filled his senses just before he lost consciousness. When he came to, which must have been only seconds later, since there were no police or ambulances there, he looked out of the crumpled door and saw the rear end of the car that had plowed into him.

A man's body was lying face down in the street, as still as death, a pool of blood deepening around his head. He couldn't make out the make and model of the other driver's car; it had rolled behind a dumpster by the side of the street.

After calling 911 on his cell phone, Ray jumped out of the passenger door. The driver's door was crushed shut so he made his way toward the body. When he got close enough, he realized breathing had stopped.

He would do CPR and pray for God's mercy. This was one of those times he was grateful to be a former street cop and for the training he had received.

He squatted down and gently turned the body over and then the awful truth of the moment hit his heart and stomach like a prize fight punch. The bloodied face with the glazed eyes belonged to his son, Bobby.

"Oh God, please no" Ray wailed as he began to blow life giving breath into Bobby's lungs while pressing on his chest.

When will that ambulance get here, he's not responding, God help me, Bobby why did you forget the seat belt? He thought as he tirelessly labored over Bobby's lifeless body. Unable to hold back the tears he wept uncontrollably as he frantically worked to save his son's life.

Bobby never opened his eyes or began to breathe on his own. There was no heartbeat, no pulse when the paramedics arrived. After securing Bobby's neck, they slid him into the back of the ambulance and without waiting for Ray to climb in beside his son, they hurriedly left for the hospital.

Ray was left standing in the street where he was approached by the officer working the accident. As soon as the officer recognized the uniform and insignia Ray was wearing and the obvious distress he was in, he realized that this was more than just an ordinary accident.

"Sir, could you answer some questions for me please? "That's my son in the ambulance, do you mind giving me a ride to the hospital and I'll answer your questions there?" Ray asked. "Not at all Sir, I'm sorry, hope he's alright. Let's go."

They arrived at the emergency room and after asking the usual questions, the officer left Ray alone in the waiting room. No one would tell him anything for the first hour but eventually the resident came out....

"Mr. Lewis, I'm Dr. Jones. Your son is alive but there's brain swelling and he's in a coma. We'll just have to wait about 48 hours to know what the prognosis is.

I'm so sorry and I wish I could give you better news but where there's life there's hope. If he has a mother, would you like for the hospital to call her?"

Still too shocked to carry on a conversation he replied, "Thank you for what you've done for Bobby but no, I'll call his mother. It will be easier for her to hear it from me."

"Whatever you prefer, and you can go in to see your son for no more than five minutes once we have him settled in ICU. I'll be in to see him periodically through the night and I've called Dr. Thomas, who is the best neurologist on staff, to examine him in the morning. Good night, Sir and I hope we will have good news soon."

Ray was a real man in every sense of the word, his broad shoulders had carried all of his responsibilities and often those of others, but this was one night being a man would be crushing.

How could he tell Cathy that their only son was lying in a coma close to death? He was sickened at the thought as he opened his cell phone and dialed.

"Hello," the soft feminine voice at the other end said then waited for him to speak.

"Cathy it's me, I have some bad news. Are you sitting down?"

"Just tell me Ray" she replied with an edge of irritation in her voice.

"There's been an accident, a car accident and Bobby is hurt. I'm at the hospital, can you drive down? I would come and get you but....well I was in the accident too and the car isn't drivable."

The other end of the phone became totally silent, he knew she was absorbing the news, she was always slow and deliberate, sensible in her reactions, but he was totally unprepared for the loud wail the pierced his ears next and the uncontrolled deep sobs.

She was overcome with fear and grief, and he wanted so badly to be there with her, to hold her close and console her.

"Cathy, Honey calm down, I'm sending a cab for you, don't want you to drive when you're this upset. I hope Bobby will be alright and I'm not hurt."

"Ray were you with Bobby? How were you involved?"

"We collided Cathy, Bobby's car is totaled and ours is bashed up bad. I'm calling that cab so be ready when it gets there. Bye Hon, will be at the Lobby door waiting for you."

There was a flurry of activity all around him, patients and families, white garbed nurses. It seemed like forever before her cab pulled up at the lobby door and she jumped out.

Her hair was in disarray, and she still wore her bedroom slippers along with jeans and a sweatshirt. Not at all like Cathy who had impeccable fashion sense. The hurry of her departure was evident.

He gently placed his arm around her shoulder and for a moment their eyes met in pain and empathy.

"Ray is he alright, what happened?"

"There was an accident Cathy and our cars collided in an intersection. I'm afraid Bobby took the brunt of the impact"

He watched in shock and disbelief as the empathy in her eyes retreated and fury crept into them like a wild beast.

"Ray you bastard, you almost killed my son. What were you doing? Absorbed in your coffee and loud music? Damn you Ray," she screamed so loudly that everyone around them stared at the drama being played out before them.

He braced himself and tried to keep a cool head and a calm voice, after all this was his son too and he hurt no less than her.

"It wasn't my fault, Cathy; Bobby ran the red light. I was already in the middle of the intersection when he hit me."

Her anger gave way to sobs and he reached out, took her in his arms and whispered assurances that it would be alright, while stroking her hair like a little girl.

For a moment he felt her body relax and lean into his but quickly she pulled away and asked to see Bobby.

They found the elevator and got off at the fifth floor ICU lobby. Todd approached the young nurse at the desk.

"We're Mr. and Mrs. Lewis, we'd like to see our son Bobby."

"Please have a seat in the waiting room Mr. Lewis, the doctor will be right out to speak with you."

They sat side by side on a leather love seat that seemed as tired as they both were. Soon Dr. Silver appeared looking even more tired than the sofa and with a concerned look on his young face.

"Mr. and Mrs. Lewis I am so sorry to tell you that the MRI has revealed significant damage to both your son's kidneys. They have shut down, are badly bruised and it's doubtful that they will recover and function properly again.

We are keeping him on dialysis until he regains consciousness, and we can evaluate the possibility of a kidney transplant. His body can function well with only one healthy kidney.

I've called in Dr. Rivas, the best urologist on the staff. There is some very good news, we have found no brain damage and when the swelling goes down, he should come out of the coma.

We need to immediately begin to evaluate any siblings and the two of you as possible kidney donors. Does Bobby have any brothers or sisters?"

"No, Bobby is our only child, and you can begin with us right away," Dr. Ray replied.

"Good we will start as soon as you spend a few minutes with him."

"Wait," Cathy said, "this is moving way too fast, just give me some time and let me see my son."

"Fine," Dr. Silver replied, "but we don't want to wait any longer than necessary to formulate our plan. If neither of you are an adequate match, we'll have to wait for a donor. Come this way and you can see him now."

Bobby lay perfectly still with tubes and wires everywhere. His handsome face was discolored and his whole head extremely swollen. Cathy took his hand in hers and wept deep, agonizing sobs.

"Oh Baby, My Poor Baby she whispered again and again until at last she responded to Ray's arm around her waist, turning and throwing herself into his arms like an injured child."

"It'll be alright, Darling, one of us will be a match and he will be good as new in no time. Now let's go they said only five minutes in here with him," Ray said as he led her away toward the waiting room.

In the empty waiting room, they sat side by side on an old leather sofa. After Cathy had wet his shirt with tears, she composed herself and looking straight into his dark-chocolate eyes with her jade ones she began to speak,

"Ray, we need to talk, there's something you need to know. There's no need for you to be tested. Bobby is...well… he's not your son."

The words hung in the air like a winter storm, darkening his whole world and it seemed as though everything was suspended, including his breath and heartbeat. He sat up straight and withdrew his hand that was covering hers.

"What are you saying Cathy, I mean….what are you saying. Bobby is another man's son. Who, why?" "Why, you want to know why? You really have no clue, do you? You think just because you love me and are kind to me when you are home, that should be enough. You remember how it was after I lost the baby? No, you probably don't, I don't think you ever really noticed.

Anyway… for a whole year after I lost the baby, I was so depressed I didn't want to live. I cried almost constantly but you weren't around much to see it, Ray.

You were working overtime and constantly out of town for training seminars. When you were home, you were preoccupied with other things most of the time.

I put on a happy face, made you dinner, made love with you and you went back to work a happy man while I struggled to stay alive."

He was pulled apart with a sense of guilt for failing her and righteous indignation at the thought she had cheated on him "Cathy, you never told me, you never let me know, I had no idea things were so bad for you. I never meant to fail you that way. Who is he, tell me, I need to know."

"Just a stranger, someone I met at the library. Someone who listened and understood my pain. It only happened twice. I needed somebody Ray, and something I wasn't getting in our marriage.

He made me feel like I was the most important thing in the universe. We met at the library every Tuesday night and afterwards we'd go for coffee. You never realized because you were either on night duty, working overtime, or out of town.

One night when he walked me home, he pulled me into the alley and before I really had any time to think about the consequences of what I was doing he had me on fire for him.

It was explosive Ray, more so than sex with you had ever been. The other time we went to his place but then I broke it off and never saw him again. I think I was in love with him, but I couldn't live with the guilt, and I didn't have enough guts to leave you.

When I realized I was pregnant I knew it wasn't yours, we hadn't been together sexually in a while, I knew it was his baby, but I just let you think it was yours, made it easier for all of us, you were too distracted to suspect the timing was off.

We won't be able to have Bobby's father tested for a kidney match. I read recently in the obituaries that he's dead. I'm glad you know. It's been a burden to carry this secret for eighteen years. So now you know, what do you plan to do?"

He sat like a stunned statue, his head bent over in his hands. A big sigh escaped from deep in his chest and through his tears he looked up and gazed into her eyes.

"The fault lies with both of us, what should I do Cathy? I'm hurt deeply and I'll confess to you that there seems to be no love or desire for me left in your heart. I was going to give you emerald earrings for Valentine's Day but was considering asking you if you would prefer a divorce instead.

So, I think we should try to support each other now and get through this. I never want Bobby to know the truth. We'll be there, with a united front for Bobby's sake and when he's recovered, we'll decide if we want that divorce."

Tears pooled in her eyes and slid down her cheeks as she whispered, "Thank you and at this point I don't think I want those earrings for Valentine's Day."

He sent her home in a cab, insisting that he should stay the night close to Bobby. There was no change and after spending the next day in the waiting room they went home that night and Ray slept in the guest room. It just seemed like the right thing to do, less emotionally draining for both.

As he lay alone in the dark, memories flooded in his mind and strong emotions his heart. Hurt and anger surrounded him at what she had done and remorse at how he had failed her. He tossed, turned, and slept little.

At the hospital the next morning, they got the news that Cathy was not a suitable match to donate a kidney but after insisting that he was tested too, the results showed that Ray was miraculously close enough that with the powerful anti-rejection drugs available, his kidney just might work.

Around noon, Dr. Rivas, a distinguished gray-haired gentleman in a white lab coat walked toward them and held out his hand to shake Ray's.

"Well, I assume you must be prepared, Mr. Lewis to donate a kidney to your son?"

"No," Cathy spoke up, "We can't assume that Dr. Rivas, Ray may need to think about it."

The expression on the doctor's face alternated between puzzlement and shock as he waited for Ray's reply.

"Of course, I'm ready to do this for my son, the sooner the better," Ray said as he took Cathy's hand in his and gave it a firm squeeze. "Great, we'll schedule it for tomorrow then."

They spent more time with Bobby that day, a special time of thankfulness and joy. The surgery was scheduled for the next day, so they went home early to rest.

Tomorrow would be Valentine's Day and Ray was proud of the gift of love he would be giving his son. Yes, Bobby was his son, he would never think of him any other way.

He lay in the darkness in the guest bedroom with only the light of a full winter's moon flooding in through the window. The small box was there on the nightstand, beautifully wrapped in pink velvet, it held the exquisite emerald and diamond earrings and matching necklace he had bought Cathy for Valentine's Day.

Tomorrow, he would give them to her along with his offer of a divorce. He reached for the box and turned it over and over in his hands, as thoughts did the same in his mind. Would she accept his offer?

Finally, sometime after midnight he fell off to sleep but sometime later was wakened by the soft warmth of her body against his back and the fragrance "White Diamonds" perfume in the air.

"Is that mine?" She asked as her hands reached out and took the velvet box from his. "Yes, it's those earrings I promised you and they are yours, even if you take my offer of a divorce."

"Forgive me," she whispered as she pressed closer to him, and he realized there was only his t-shirt and boxers between him and her bare skin. "Forgive me too, Honey. I'll never be distant and uncaring to you again."

"In that case, she replied, as she nuzzled his neck and the fullness of her breasts pressed tightly into his back. "I'll take the earrings, and a night of love."

Tears filled his eyes as he turned to face her. She was stunning in the soft moonlight, as beautiful as she had been the first time, they made love so many years before

"Happy Valentine's Day," he whispered as he took her tenderly in his arms and kissed her with more fire than any other man ever could have.

Chapter 30

The Disabled Athlete

It isn't nice to tell a disabled person what to do. They will go into shock or even into an episode that you will regret it in time...

"I already suffered from depression and anxiety and that's been made worse by Corona so now I'm fearful and cry a lot. I'm worried about my family members will die, and I'm scared because it feels like a zombie apocalypse."

"I'm a disabled athlete with a visual impairment and am usually very active. I attend swimming training three times a week and I go to goalball, a blind Paralympic sport, competitions and training up and down the country a few times a month.

I must miss my weekly art classes, and I generally miss the routine of attending school.

I miss being active, attending goalball training and tournaments. My goalball coaching sessions with younger children are great.

Sport helps my mental health so I really miss it when I can't do it. I'm also sad I've had two concerts and many theatre trips cancelled.

My parents are trying very hard to keep me active. We do our daily walk and mom and dad come up with things to keep me interested.

We like having a cinema experience at home, so we'll buy a film on Sky box office and have a big box of popcorn.

My mom arranged with my art tutor to continue sessions via FaceTime. I'm doing baking, drawing, puzzles and playing with my cats.

I am trying so hard to fit in the mainstream, however, doctors and teachers told my parents that it is not recommended.

Chapter 31

Sexual abuse in School

Sexual abuse in primary and secondary schools' concerns child sexual abuse, occurring in educational institutions from kindergarten through secondary education.

Sexual assault is any kind of sexual activity that you were forced, or tricked into doing when you did not want to.

It refers to a wide range of unwanted sexual behaviors including forced sex, unwanted sex, sexual acts or touching.

Child sexual abuse: using power over a child or adolescent to involve them in sexual activity. Indecent assault: touching, or threatening to touch, someone else's body sexually without their consent.

With teachers having much influence and proximity to children, sexual abuse in schools occurs at high rates.

A 1993 study performed by the American Association of University Women examined seventy-nine state schools in the United States and found that 9.6% of students reported sexual abuse by teachers in the school setting.

The victims of school sexual abuse are often "vulnerable or marginal students"

Primary prevention has been identified as a priority in challenging sexual violence, but there is a lack of understanding around what primary prevention is and is not.

Although increasing knowledge or awareness of sexual assault may be a feature of primary prevention, it is not a sufficient outcome. Primary prevention must also change behaviors. Some work has been done on identifying the elements required for effective primary prevention.

These include comprehensiveness, community engagement, theory-driven programming, contextualized programming, and evaluation.

By 1988, prevention programs and materials about school sexual abuse came into vogue.

Problems associated with these, however, include "emphasizing a simple solution to a complex social problem and contributing to victim blaming."

Despite the prevalence of these prevention programs and materials, multiple studies have demonstrated that "teachers use programs spasmodically and selectively, omitting the essential concepts relating to children's rights".

Child sexual abuse can result in both short-term and long-term harm, including psychopathology in later life.

Indicators and effects include depression, anxiety, eating disorders, poor self-esteem, somatization, sleep disturbances, and dissociative and anxiety disorders including post-traumatic stress disorder.

While children may exhibit regressive behaviors such as thumb sucking or bedwetting, the strongest indicator of sexual abuse is sexual acting out and inappropriate sexual knowledge and interest.

Victims may withdraw from school and social activities and exhibit various learning and behavioral problems including cruelty to animals, attention deficit/hyperactivity disorder (ADHD), conduct disorder, and oppositional defiant disorder (ODD).

Teenage pregnancy and risky sexual behaviors may appear in adolescence.[39] Child sexual abuse victims report almost four times as many incidences of self-inflicted harm.

A study funded by the USA National Institute of Drug Abuse found that "Among more than 1,400 adult females, childhood sexual abuse was associated with increased likelihood of drug dependence, alcohol dependence, and psychiatric disorders.

The associations are expressed as odds ratios: for example, women who experienced congenital sexual abuse in childhood were 2.83 times more likely to suffer drug dependence as adults than were women who were not abused."

A well-documented, long-term negative effect is repeated or additional victimization in adolescence and adulthood.

A causal relationship has been found between childhood sexual abuse and various adult psychopathologies, including crime and suicide, in addition to alcoholism and drug abuse.

Males who were sexually abused as children more frequently appear in the criminal justice system than in a clinical mental health setting.

A study comparing middle-aged women who were abused as children with non-abused counterparts found significantly higher health care costs for the former.

Intergenerational effects have been noted, with the children of victims of child sexual abuse exhibiting more conduct problems, peer problems, and emotional problems than their peers.

A specific characteristic pattern of symptoms has not been identified, and there are several hypotheses about the causality of these associations.

Studies have found that 51% to 79% of sexually abused children exhibit psychological symptoms. The risk of harm is greater if the abuser is a relative, if the abuse involves intercourse or attempted intercourse, or if threats or force are used.

The level of harm may also be affected by various factors such as penetration, duration and frequency of abuse, and use of force.

The social stigma of child sexual abuse may compound the psychological harm to children, and adverse outcomes are less likely for abused children who have supportive family environments.

Chapter 32

Revelation

Children who received supportive responses following disclosure had less traumatic symptoms and were abused for a shorter period than children who did not receive support.

In general, studies have found that children need support and stress-reducing resources after disclosure of sexual abuse.

Negative social reactions to disclosure have been found to be harmful to the survivor's well-being.

One study reported that children who received a bad reaction from the first person they told, especially if the person was a close family member, had worse scores as adults on general trauma symptoms, post-traumatic stress disorder symptoms, and dissociation.

Another study found that in most cases when children did disclose abuse, the person they talked to did not respond effectively, blamed, or rejected the child, and took little or no action to stop the abuse.

Non-validating and otherwise non-supportive responses to disclosure by the child's primary attachment figure may indicate a relational disturbance predating the sexual abuse that may have been a risk factor for the abuse, and which can remain a risk factor for its psychological consequences.

The American Academy of Child and Adolescent Psychiatry provides guidelines for what to say to the victim and what to do following the disclosure.

Asa Don Brown has indicated: "A minimization of the trauma and its effects is commonly injected into the picture by parental caregivers to shelter and calm the child. It has been commonly assumed that focusing on children's issues too long will negatively impact their recovery.

Therefore, the parental caregiver teaches the child to mask his or her issues."

In many jurisdictions, abuse that is suspected, not necessarily proven, requires reporting to child protection agencies, such as the Child Protection Services in the United States.

Recommendations for healthcare workers, such as primary care providers and nurses, who are often suited to encounter suspected abuse are advised to firstly determine the child's immediate need for safety.

A private environment away from suspected abusers is desired for interviewing and examination. Leading statements that can distort the story are avoided.

As revealing abuse can be distressing and sometimes even shameful, reassuring the child that he or she has done the right thing by telling and that they are not bad and that the abuse was not their fault helps in disclosing more information.

Anatomically correct dolls are sometimes used to help explain what happened, although some researchers consider the dolls too explicit and overstimulating, which might contribute to non-abused children behaving with the dolls in one or more ways that suggest they were sexually abused.

For the suspected abusers, it is also recommended to use a nonjudgmental, nonthreatening attitude towards them and to withhold expressing shock, to help disclose information.

Chapter 33

Adults

Adults who have been sexually abused as children often present for treatment with a secondary mental health issue, which can include substance abuse, eating disorders, personality disorders, depression, and conflict in romantic or interpersonal relationships.

Generally, the approach is to focus on the present problem, rather than the abuse itself. Treatment is highly varied and depends on the person's specific issues. For instance, a person with a history of sexual abuse and severe depression would be treated for depression.

However, there is often an emphasis on cognitive restructuring due to the deep-seated nature of the trauma. Some newer techniques such as eye movement desensitization and reprocessing, EMDR, have been shown to be effective.

Although there is no known cure for pedophilia, there are several treatments for pedophiles and child sexual abusers.

Some of the treatments focus on attempting to change the sexual preference of pedophiles, while others focus on keeping pedophiles from committing child sexual abuse, or on keeping child sexual abusers from committing child sexual abuse again.

Cognitive behavioral therapy CBT, for example, aims to reduce attitudes, beliefs, and behaviors that may increase the likelihood of sexual offenses against children.

Its content varies widely between therapists, but a typical program might involve training in self-control, social competence, and empathy, and use cognitive restructuring to change views on sex with children.

The most common form of this therapy is relapse prevention, where the patient is taught to identify and respond to potentially risky situations based on principles used for treating addictions.

The evidence for cognitive behavioral therapy is mixed.

A 2012 Cochrane Review of randomized trials found that CBT had no effect on risk of reoffending for contact sex offenders.

Meta-analyses in 2002 and 2005, which included both randomized and non-randomized studies, concluded that CBT reduced recidivism.

There is debate over whether non-randomized studies should be considered informative.

Sexual abuse is associated with many sub-clinical behavioral issues as well, including re-victimization in the teenage years, a bipolar-like switching between sexual compulsion and shut-down, and distorted thinking about sexual abuse, for instance, that it is common and happens to everyone.

When first presenting for treatment, the patient can be fully aware of their abuse as an event, but their appraisal of it is often distorted, such as believing that the event was unremarkable, a form of isolation.

Frequently, victims do not make the connection between their abuse and their present pathology.

Chapter 34

Prevention Programs

My sister and I used to meet once a week to talk about each situation. I used to work in Brooklyn, NY and she used to work in Long Island. We were both teachers, therefore it was easy talking to her. We tried to make a difference in the public school system.

Child sexual abuse prevention programs were developed in the United States of America during the 1970s.

Some programs are delivered to children and can include one-to-one work and group work.

Programs delivered to parents were developed in the 1980s and took the form of one-off meetings, two to three hours long.

In the last 15 years, web-based programs have been developed. School-based education programs were evaluated in 2015 by Cochrane that demonstrated improvements in protective behaviors and knowledge among children.

Chapter 35

United States and Europe

Child sexual abuse occurs frequently in Western society, although the rate of prevalence can be difficult to determine. Research in North America has concluded that approximately 15% to 25% of women and 5% to 15% of men were sexually abused when they were children.

In the UK, a 2010 study estimated prevalence at about 5% for boys and 18% for girls, not dissimilar to a 1985 study that estimated about 8% for boys and 12% for girls. More than 23,000 incidents were recorded by the UK police between 2009 and 2010.

Girls were six times more likely to be assaulted than boys with 86% of attacks taking place against them.

Barnardo's charity estimates that two thirds of victims in the United Kingdom are girls and one third are boys. Barnardo's is concerned that boy victims may be overlooked.

A firm of solicitors that acts in many cases of child abuse has published a list of over twenty Children's Homes and group actions that they have an interest in or for which they are lead solicitors.

The estimates for the United States vary widely. A literature review of 23 studies found rates of 3% to 37% for males and 8% to 71% for females, which produced an average of 17% for boys and 28% for girls, while a statistical analysis based on 16 cross-sectional studies estimated the rate to be 7.2% for males and 14.5% for females.

The US Department of Health and Human Services reported 83,600 substantiated reports of sexually abused children in 2005,while state-level child protective services reported 63,527 sexual abuse incidents in 2010. Including incidents which were not reported would make the total number even larger.

According to Emily M. Douglas and David Finkelor, "Several national studies have found that black and white children experienced near-equal levels of sexual abuse. Other studies, however, have found that both blacks and Latinos have an increased risk for sexual victimization".

Surveys have shown that one fifth to one third of all women reported some sort of childhood sexual experience with a male adult.

A 1992 survey studying father-daughter incest in Finland reported that of the 9,000 15-year-old high school girls who filled out the questionnaires, of the girls living with their biological fathers, 0.2% reported father-daughter incest experiences; of the girls living with a stepfather, 3.7% reported sexual experiences with him.

The reported counts included only father-daughter incest and did not include prevalence of other forms of child sexual abuse. The survey summary stated, "the feelings of the girls about their incestual experiences are overwhelmingly negative."

Others argue that prevalence rates are much higher, and that many cases of child abuse are never reported. One study found that professionals failed to report approximately 40% of the child sexual abuse cases they encountered.

A study by Lawson & Chaffin indicated that many children who were sexually abused were "identified solely by a physical complaint that was later diagnosed as a venereal disease ... Only 43% of the children who were diagnosed with venereal disease made a verbal disclosure of sexual abuse during the initial interview."

It has been found in the epidemiological literature on CSA that there is no identifiable demographic or family characteristic of a child that can be used to bar the prospect that a child has been sexually abused.

Child marriage is often considered to be another form of child sexual abuse.

Over 200,000 marriages involving minors were allowed between 2000 and 2015 in the US. These marriages were most often between an adult male and female minor.

Child marriage in the United States is allowed in most of the states as long as parental consent or judicial approval, typically for pregnancy, is given.

In US schools, according to the United States Department of Education, "nearly 9.6% of students are targets of educator sexual misconduct sometime during their school career.

"In studies of student sex abuse by male and female educators, male students were reported as targets in ranges from 23% to 44%.

In U.S. school settings same-sex, female and male, sexual misconduct against students by educators "ranges from 18 to 28% of reported cases, depending on the study"

Significant underreporting of sexual abuse of boys by both women and men is believed to occur due to sex stereotyping, social denial, the minimization of male victimization, and the relative lack of research on sexual abuse of boys.

Sexual victimization of boys by their mothers or other female relatives is especially rarely researched or reported. Sexual abuse of girls by their mothers, and other related and/or unrelated adult females is beginning to be researched and reported despite the highly taboo nature of female–female child sex abuse. In studies where students are asked about sex offenses, they report higher levels of female sex offenders than found in adult reports.

This underreporting has been attributed to cultural denial of female-perpetrated child sex abuse, because "males have been socialized to believe they should be flattered or appreciative of sexual interest from a female.

"Journalist Cathy Young writes that under-reporting is contributed to by the difficulty of people, including jurors, in seeing a male as a "true victim".

In the United Kingdom, reported child sex abuse has increased, but this may be due to greater willingness to report. Police need more resources to deal with it. Also, parents and schools need to give children and adolescents regular advice about how to spot abuse and about the need to report abuse.

Software providers are urged to do more to police their environment and make it safe for children.

Child sexual abuse is outlawed nearly everywhere in the world, generally with severe criminal penalties, including in some jurisdictions, life imprisonment or capital punishment.

An adult's sexual intercourse with someone below the legal age of consent is defined as statutory rape, based on the principle that a child is not capable of consent and that any apparent consent by a child is not considered to be legal consent.

The United Nations Convention on the Rights of the Child (CRC) is an international treaty that legally obliges states to protect children's rights. Articles 34 and 35 of the CRC require states to protect children from all forms of sexual exploitation and sexual abuse.

This includes outlawing the coercion of a child to perform sexual activity, the prostitution of children, and the exploitation of children in creating pornography. States are also required to prevent the abduction, sale, or trafficking of children.

As of November 2008, 193 countries are bound by the CRC, including every member of the United Nations except the United States and South Sudan.

The Council of Europe has adopted the Council of Europe Convention on the Protection of Children against Sexual Exploitation and Sexual Abuse in order to prohibit child sexual abuse that occurs within home or family.

In the European Union, child sexual abuse is subject to a directive. This directive deals with several forms of sexual abuse of children, especially commercial sexual exploitation of children.

Child sexual abuse has gained public attention since the 1970s and has become one of the most high-profile crimes. While sexual use of children by adults has been present throughout history, public interest in prevention has tended to fluctuate.

Initially, concern centered around children under the age of ten, but over time, advocates have attracted attention toward the sexual abuse of children between the ages of 11 and 17.

Up until the 1930s, the psychological impact of sexual abuse was not emphasized, instead emphasis was placed on the physical harm or the child's reputation.[246] Widespread public awareness of children's sexual abuse did not occur until the 1970s in the West.

The first published work dedicated specifically to child sexual abuse appeared in France in 1857: Medical-Legal Studies of Sexual Assault, Etude Médico-Légale sur les Attentats aux Mœurs, by Auguste Ambroise Tardieu, the noted French pathologist and pioneer of forensic medicine.

Child sexual abuse became a public issue in the 1970s and 1980s. Prior to this point in time, sexual abuse remained rather secretive and socially unspeakable.

Studies on child molestation were nonexistent until the 1920s and the first national estimate of the number of child sexual abuse cases was published in 1948.

By 1968 44 out of 50 U.S. states had enacted mandatory laws that required physicians to report cases of suspicious child abuse. Legal action began to become more prevalent in the 1970s with the enactment of the Child Abuse Prevention and Treatment Act in 1974 in conjunction with the creation of the National Center for Child Abuse and Neglect. Since the creation of the Child Abuse and Treatment Act, reported child abuse cases have increased dramatically. Finally, the National Abuse Coalition was created in 1979 to create pressure in congress to create more sexual abuse laws.

Second wave feminism brought greater awareness of child sexual abuse and violence against women, and made them public, political issues.

Judith Lewis Herman, Harvard professor of psychiatry, wrote the first book ever on father-daughter incest when she discovered during her medical residency that many the women, she was seeing had been victims of father-daughter incest.

Herman notes that her approach to her clinical experience grew out of her involvement in the civil rights movement.

Her second book Trauma and Recovery coined the term complex post-traumatic stress disorder and included child sexual abuse as a cause.

In 1986, Congress passed the Child Abuse Victims' Rights Act, giving children a civil claim in sexual abuse cases. The number of laws created in the 1980s and 1990s began to create greater prosecution and detection of child sexual abusers.

During the 1970s a large transition began in the legislature related to child sexual abuse. Megan's Law who was enacted in 1996 gives the public access to knowledge of sex offenders nationwide.

Anne Hastings described these changes in attitudes towards child sexual abuse as "the beginning of one of history's largest social revolutions."

According to John Jay College of Criminal Justice professor B.J. Cling,

"By the early 21st century, the issue of child sexual abuse has become a legitimate focus of professional attention, while increasingly separated from second wave feminism ...

As child sexual abuse becomes absorbed into the larger field of interpersonal trauma studies, child sexual abuse studies and intervention strategies have become degendered and largely unaware of their political origins in modern feminism and other vibrant political movements of the 1970s.

One may hope that unlike in the past, this rediscovery of child sexual abuse that began in the 70s will not again be followed by collective amnesia. The institutionalization of child maltreatment interventions in federally funded centers, national and international societies, and a host of research studies, in which the United States continues to lead the world, offers grounds for cautious optimism. Nevertheless, as Judith Herman argues cogently,

'The systematic study of psychological trauma ... depends on the support of a political movement.'

Chapter 36

Civil lawsuits

In the United States growing awareness of child sexual abuse has sparked an increasing number of civil lawsuits for monetary damages stemming from such incidents.

Increased awareness of child sexual abuse has encouraged more victims to come forward, whereas in the past victims often kept their abuse secret.

Some states have enacted specific laws lengthening the applicable statutes of limitations to allow victims of child sexual abuse to file suit sometimes years after they have reached the age of majority.

Such lawsuits can be brought where a person or entity, such as a school, church or youth organization, or daycare was charged with supervising the child but failed to do so with child sexual abuse resulting, making the individual or institution liable.

In the Catholic sex abuse cases the various Roman Catholic Diocese in the United States have paid out approximately $1 billion settling hundreds of such lawsuits since the early 1990s.

There have also been lawsuits involving the American religious right. Crimes have allegedly gone unreported, and victims were pressured into silence.

As lawsuits can involve demanding procedures there is a concern that children or adults who file suit will be re-victimized by defendants through the legal process, much as rape victims can be re-victimized by the accused in criminal rape trials. The child sexual abuse plaintiff's attorney Thomas A. Cifarelli has written that children involved in the legal system, particularly victims of sexual abuse and molestation, should be afforded certain procedural safeguards to protect them from harassment during the legal process.

In June 2008, in Zambia the issue of teacher-student sexual abuse and sexual assault was brought to the attention of the High Court of Zambia where a landmark case decision, with presiding Judge Philip Musonda, awarded $45million Zambian kwacha, US$13,000, to the plaintiff, a 13-year-old girl for sexual abuse and rape by her schoolteacher.

This claim was brought against her teacher as a "person of authority" who, as Judge Musonda stated, "had a moral superiority, responsibility, over his students" at the time.

Chapter 37

The Innocent

A small boy was alone, playing outside, when the police officers showed up. The boy was six years old. He was pretending to be an outlaw, taking life and land from the innocent.

A black jeep came down the driveway. Gravel crunched under the tires. The boy lived in a dry, rural countryside, in the Catskills of up state Mountains. He considered himself to be a Man, tough and harsh lawless.

He didn't understand that he lived in a homeowner's association. One that was developed in the middle mountains. The houses were spaced far apart by city standards and packed together by country standards. It was the suburbs with property. This was a place to get away from the cities and their people.

There was a nine-hole golf course with a restaurant on site. A gas station. There was clubhouse with a swimming pool, tennis courts, and a bar & grill. Homeowners paid their dues to live in this community. It was a sheltered place to grow up.

The police officers parked their jeep and got out. In the back of the jeep was a German Shepard. It was barking. Saliva flew from its mouth. Chunks of saliva spotted the reinforced glass window.

The uniformed men, with guns hanging from their hips, greeted the boy and asked him where his father was. There was pity in their eyes.

The boy gestured toward his house. He pointed the way with one hand while he sucked on the fingers of the other.

The men departed toward the home. The boy was left alone. He stared at the black jeep. Inside the jeep, the dog was still barking.

The word Police was painted in blue letters on the side of the vehicle. The boy didn't understand the word. The dog continued to bark.

The two police officers came out of the house. The boy's father was between them, hands at his sides. His mother was behind the three men. She was crying. The father said something to the police officers. They nodded solemnly.

The father came over to the boy and kneeled. He told him that he loved him and that he'd be back, but for now he had to go away. The boy was going to be the Man of The House for a while. He would need to be tough.

Okay, he replied, but he didn't understand.

The father took his cap off and placed it on the boy's head.

The police officers escorted him to the jeep. The barking grew unbearably loud as the door opened. It returned to its muffled volume when the door slammed closed on his father.

The police officers looked at the boy and his mother. They nodded. One of them was stiff-jawed and holding back moisture in his eyes. The other was somber. They left.

The jeep backed up the driveway. The gravel crunched and groaned under the weight of the tires. The jeep, and all inside, drove away. The barking faded.

The boy looked to his mother. He asked her where they were taking his father.

She told him they were taking him away, so that he could take care of his own father, who was very sick.

He didn't understand that she was lying.

Okay, he replied.

He saw his father three more times after his mother obtained custody of him and his brother. He started thinking of his father as someone else, some lawless villain, some stranger. Two of the visits were in a small booth. He could see the man through the clear, reinforced glass and he could speak to him through a phone receiver.

The third visit was in an open-air courtyard. They sat at a grey concrete table surrounded by tall, grey, concrete walls. There were other families at other concrete tables. There were uniformed men, with guns hanging from their hips, standing solemnly, their hands folded in front. Their backs were against tall, grey walls. They watched the families, or what used to be families.

The boy later found out why his father was taken away, that his father had committed crimes against children.

The man would write to the boy every birthday, but the boy never answers.

He couldn't communicate with the man. The man who may have hurt him. He wasn't sure. He couldn't remember if anything happened.

All the boy could remember about his childhood was the day that the police officer came to his house. That was the day that man was taken away. It was the last day the boy pretended to be an outlaw.

Chapter 38

Not a Bit Blind

She can't explain to you what she sees. She doesn't know what she sees when she closes her eyes…

Every night at the same time, her father would come into her room. It's always very dark. The fragile little girl would always close her eyes. She tried to explain to her psychologist that when she closes her eyes, she sees the same thing as when they're open.

She sees nothing. She doesn't think it's black, or dark. She can't explain or doesn't want to…

The school phycologist kept asking so many questions. The little girl by the way is 12 years old. She was very naïve and abused by her father.

In one of her sessions, she tried to explain that she cannot see. She knows she is not blind.

The psychologist kept repeating, if you can't explain to me what black or dark is, then you should understand when I say I can't explain what you see and don't see.

The little girl who I named her Milagros, meaning miracle, will begin trusting me as her home room teacher and the rest of the special Ed staff…

She began talking:

I can't explain to you what it's like living with my father.

Whenever I heard kids at school talk about getting grounded and not being allowed out of their room, I would just nod my head and wonder what they did about the stink.

After a full day of using the plastic garbage can in the corner for a toilet, placing a pillow over the top would cover the smell, but after two or three days, nothing could stop that stench from filling the room. Some smells go away the more you smell them, but not that. It took me a while to realize that they were talking about something totally different.

So maybe there are a lot of things that I'm missing, that I'll never see. How do you know that there isn't a whole world out there that you're missing too? What if there's a whole universe out there that you just can't understand because you're not tuned in to it, because you don't have the right senses for it?

I don't know what a sunrise looks like, but I've felt its warmth coming through the slats of my bedroom window, or in the car on the way to school, or waking me up in the mornings that I slept in the backyard because my father had locked me out the night before. I don't know what my best friend's face looks like, but I remember what her voice sounded like when she asked me where I'd been all week and I told her I was sick, and she said, "Again?"

I don't know what a bruise looks like, but I know that there were days that I asked my teachers if I could just stand in the back of the room instead of sitting because it felt more comfortable. Or days when even the book bag slung over my shoulder brushing against my arm sent dull pain through it down to the bone.

I've never seen any of my teachers, but I'm not sure any of them have seen me either. Maybe they think that sweatshirts and jackets in May are a blind thing.

I've never seen my father either, but I've felt him many times. I know the weight of his hand, the hardness of his fist, the grip in his fingers. I know the smell of him after he's come home from work with sour sweat and oil all over him.

I know the smell of him after he's come home from a weekend gone, the metallic, wretched smell of blood and dirt and vomit.

You know how you can feel someone standing behind you even if they don't make a sound? Or when you know someone is on the other side of a door, even if they don't answer when you knock? Or the sense that the person you're talking to is really two people? Or three or more, and some not like people at all?

I tried so hard to ask my mother how to come she never helped....

I was terrified when my father came home from a weekend out. It feels like I go from being all alone in the house to standing in the school hallways between classes. Nobody touches me, nobody speaks to me, but there's that sense of being surrounded. Do you know that feeling?

At school it's like I'm a ghost. I wander through the halls, right hand on the wall, feeling the cold of the paint abruptly turn into the cold of the metal lockers and the heat of the bodies flowing around me on the left but never touching me, never speaking. My teachers talk to me when necessary, so at least I know I'm real.

You're the first person to ever ask me about my life, what it's like to be me. Even my friend doesn't ask. She mostly talks about herself, and then when I say something about me, she acts weird, or just keeps talking, like she didn't hear me.

Fine, I guess? About the same as anyone else. There are good days when I have the house to myself and there's either food in the fridge or money in the drawer to get some. Then there's bad days. Like everyone, I guess.

I get it. I can't see you either, but I can feel you looking at the clock on the wall. Plus, you've been writing, obviously, but you haven't said anything for a while. Thanks for taking the time to ask about me, and I'll be sure to get my grades back up. In fact, I should probably be getting back to class.

Milagros did get her life back. She graduated with honors in high school and then to college.

She is presently teaching in New York City....

Chapter 39

The Hand

The hand is what Mary remembers. Its warmth on her skin. The soft skin hidden within the curve of her thigh. The place she likes to fold her own hand at night.

It feels cozy, warm, and very comforting. It feels very safe. She doesn't know how to explain about this other hand being there. It's just there. Like the memory itself is just there.

It reminds her of helping grandad move after her grandma died. There were boxes and boxes of paintings and old books, decorated pot plants, little mother-of-pearl bowls nestled in thick swathes of newspapers, and a huge Japanese fan. She was amazed.

"Where's all this stuff come from?" Mary asked her dad.

"What are you talking about?" He answered. "It's always been here."

And so, it had. She looked around and saw the outline the fan had left on the wall, the dents in the carpet made by the pots and the pale-yellow rings on the side table where the bowls had sat, immobile, for years.

This memory feels like that. She can remember it, but she has never looked at it. She never wanted to. There are some objects you want to blend in, to become part of the furniture.

"What can you see?" the hypnotherapist asks.

Mary scrunches her eyes even more firmly shut.

"Nothing," she replies.

She can hear her re-crossing her legs. The whisper of cloth rubbing against cloth and the creak of the chair as she shifts from one side to the other.

She asked Mary when she came in where she would like to sit. Where she would feel the most comfortable…

Mary was excited that at last, after two sessions of just talking, they were going to try some actual hypnosis.

Mary chose the armchair opposite the window. She liked the old-fashioned flower print, partially covered by a purple plaid. Soft and velvety to the touch. She strokes it now, burying her fingers into its folds.

Her hands are sticky…

"Let's go back to the cot," she says. "What does that remind you? Anything at all?"

A hand. That is what I remember. A hand that presses into the fabric between my legs while I pretend to be asleep.

Mary shift in her chair. "I'm not sure how this is going to help me stop smoking," she say.

She can hear the accusing tone in her voice.

"Are my questions making you feel uncomfortable?" she asks.

"No," Mary answers.

At the end, she tells her about seeing my cat get run over by a tractor. How she then couldn't sleep without a night light until well into her teens.

Mary pays her, thank her and book another appointment. She already knew she won't go. she'll find another way to quit smoking.

But she can't forget…

I hesitate once. A few months later. It's Christmas. I'm helping Mum prepare the plates in the kitchen. I'm arranging the roast potatoes into neat trios while she finishes cutting the goose. I nearly say:

"Mom, did you ever hire a babysitter when I was a kid? Say, before the age of four?"

But I swallow the words with a gulp of wine because the worst that could happen, the absolute worst that could happen, is if she answered: "no".

Chapter 40

The Runaway Duet

Armando timed it perfectly...

He opened the front door just now his mother threw a picture frame hitting the wall right behind his dad.

Neither Armando nor his sister heard his father leave. He learned early to get out unnoticed when he wasn't the focus of his parents' violence, when they were just beating the hell out of each other and not him or his sister.

Jean, five years old and as weary of violence as her big brother, followed him from her seat on the porch. They went around to the big dogwood that covered up the living room window,

They sat on the furthest side facing the dirt road. It was a fine Southern night. There were no clouds, just a small updraft of a breeze. A high moon bouncing light right at the kids.

When parents were calm, you could hear the deep, natural country quiet out here in this part of the woods. The only good thing out here, in either sibling's opinion.

Armando tried to focus on the sky and not the drafty, angry wooden house behind him. Jean put her head on Armando's shoulder. He adjusted his arm, wrapped it around her tiny body. "I'm so sick of their shit," Jean said.

Armando only aged nine, agreed with her.

Inside, something heavier than a picture frame hit the wall, landing with a thump. His mother screamed in pain. His father demanded her to shut up and stay down.

Jean shifted in his embrace, put a mutilated hand on his arm. Those broken fingers hadn't ever healed right. "Why haven't we run away ?"

He stopped. It was the first time she'd ever asked him that. She didn't remember when she was a baby. He a new witness to his parents' general rage, tried to run.

They followed his small shoeless footprints in the dirt road, caught him two miles away. He had bruises for three weeks, and never complained about Jean's crying ever again. But now... "I don't know, sis," he whispered. "I don't think we ought to."

"Well, I'm going to. Just because they're crazy it doesn't mean I am." She put pressure on his leg to stand up, then put one foot in front of the other. Her dirty dress swished around her as her little feet moved through the grass.

"Jean, no." She turned back to him. "Not the dirt road. They'll see."

She walked towards him. He thought she would sit down beside him. They will wait until the fight is over. They will slip back inside the house.

They just two good kids that never made too much noise because neither parent liked it.

Armando and Jean were afraid of those two parents...

Jean little feet were ready to run. Armando decided to stop her from running.

Armando's eyes went wide as she stopped midair. Her left foot held in place about seven inches off the ground. Jean mumbled with effort, and her right foot came up, landing over a foot above the left.

"Come on, Armando," she whispered, low and urgent. "It's just like stairs. The best ones yet."

He had questions. He had fears. He had nightmares about what they'd do if they get caught.

Suddenly, they heard a sharp sound from inside the house. Armando stopped worrying. He got up and ran after her, foot rising in the exact same place. He was stepping on nothing, no texture on his soles, just a slight sinking feeling.

He imagined stepping on a large, invisible marshmallow, big enough to hold him, but not so big he wouldn't leave an imprint. It was the first time he'd laughed in weeks.

One foot after the other. Up and up. The dirty shack's roof, with its freckling of unpatched shingles letting in the night sky, was visible after a bit. He stopped looking back. Jean was so brave; she hadn't looked back at all.

For long bits of sky, they didn't rise. They just ran level, like it was ground. Jean kept ahead for the most part. Sometimes Armando caught up with her. Jean gains the lead again.

The moon and stars seemed to get brighter the higher up they went, way past the treetops, nearing a cave opening towards Mount Horton's peak.

Armando had no idea how long they'd been running. "Hey, Jean, you think we need to run, or can we just walk?"

She stopped, thinking. Her next step was slower, hesitant. It didn't go up as high, but it went. "I think it's better if we run, but we can walk if you need to."

Armando shook his head. "I'm not tired. I can run all into the night."

"Race you."

"Where to? There isn't much to call a finish line up here."

Jean's head tilted around, stopping on a cloud formation. She pointed. "See that cloud there, the one that looks like a bell? I bet I can get there first."

Both siblings left their home on a beautiful summer night. Their parents never noticed that they ran away....

They were rescued by some nearby neighbors.

Chapter 41

The Abusers' Parents

The crimes were recounted for the first time in a District Court...

After 14 years of their abuse being kept secret, a father was on trial for more than 80 child sex offences. A mother was also on trial with over 20 different charges.

The father, a truck driver, raped his daughter for the first time when the mother was giving birth to their second child. The fragile little girl was only five.

Over that same year, the father continued sexually and physically abusing her in a shed near their family home.

Many nights, the girl would be tied and left in the shed. When she grew older, she would be locked inside a tiny box.

During those times, she was left unfed and forced to miss school. When her siblings asked where she was, the father would lie saying she was at a friend's house.

According to some documents, the court outlines that the daughter grew up desperately wanting to please her father, particularly on "special days".

One "special day" was Father's Day, and after bringing him breakfast in bed, the father forced her to perform sexual acts on him.

The abuse continued to become more savage as the girl participated in national sporting events. This happened often when she did not perform up to the standards her father desired.

The shed became a house of horrors, where she was raped and mutilated with tools....

By the age of 14, the father became worried she would fall pregnant and so began giving her birth control pills. He told his other children that they were vitamins.

Throughout all of this, the mother ignored the sexual abuses. She lied to her daughter by telling her that her father was doing what was best.

At 17, she tried to take her life…

The beginning of her road to escape occurred when she told her teacher that she was inappropriately touched.

From there, she was in and out of mental health clinics, with her parents often preventing her from seeking help.

At the age of 18, she was discharged from a clinic and never returned home.

Unfortunately, during a meeting with her siblings, her father turned up where he proceeded to drag her into a car and rape her.

As he raped her, he said, "How dare you tell people, you're a liar. I've only ever tried to be a good dad."

He only released her when she promised to come home, but instead she returned to a mental health clinic and for the first time, she told the police.

Despite an apprehended violence order application being taken out against her parents, her father would continue to follow her, until one time he grabbed her again and tied her.

She was taken back to the family home. Before she could be further abused, she escaped and called the police. It was then that her parents were arrested.

The shed was found by police, and inside they discovered a scene filled with blood, tools, and scratching on the walls, detailing her abuse.

After a 12-week trial, the father was found guilty on all counts. The mother was found guilty on 13 of the 16 offences against her.

I find it disgusting that the "mother" in this situation got lesser charges than the father. As far as I'm concerned if someone stands by and let's something like this happen, they are just as guilty as the criminal.

Chapter 42

The Nightmare

Jessenia was 8 years old when her father started sexually abusing her. Her mother, Rita, cries as she tells the Special Education staff how she found out.

"My daughter was crying when she told me she didn't want her dad to come to the house... she said he was mean and then told me" Mom, I am going to tell you something. Every time Dad comes back from his trips, he abuses me."

Jessenia was 13 when she told her mom for the first time. The abuse had been going on for 5 years.

Still just a child, Jessenia was paralyzed with fear. "When those things happened, I could have chosen the easiest solution and committed suicide, but I didn't. No, I pressed on, I had my brother." Jessenia refers to Leroy her younger brother and best friend who has a hearing disability and cannot speak.

It took courage to tell her mother, and Jessenia's bravery paid off.

After she told her mother, they gathered all their courage and confronted Jessenia's father.

That night, her dad ran off into the darkness, never to come back again. Rita then reported the abuse to the local authorities.

Jessenia has dealt with great anxiety and nightmares. With so many years of horrific abuse, it will take time to truly be healed. Jessenia was assigned a social worker, Audrey, who recounts parts of her journey....

"One day, it was pouring outside, the rain was so strong, but Jessica's commitment to healing was stronger. Despite the crazy rain, Jessenia showed up at the office. I still remember she was completely wet, her hair was dripping, her clothes were completely damp, but she showed up!"

Today, Jessenia is positive and hopeful about the future of her family. She is studying special education, inspired by her younger brother, Leroy. She has learned how to sign and is even teaching her mother how to sign.

Jessica and her mother Rita are now going around the 50 states visiting schools. They had helped thousands of abusive children. Their message has been heard....

Chapter 43

What happened to Sandy?

Sandy's story is one of our most memorable from my years as a special ed teacher. I want to warn you that her story contains suggestions to sexual assault and may be hard to read.

The three men who raped Sandy threatened Sandy and her little brother to keep her quiet. Confused and terrified, this brave child did the only thing she knew how to do to protect herself and the brother she loved.

Months later, Sandy's mother was shocked to discover that her 11-year-old daughter was pregnant.

At last, the terrible truth came out, and Sandy's mother did exactly what I would have done. She went straight to the authorities.

Once, a girl like Sandy could not have hoped for justice. Why, because Sandy was illegal.

Thanks to compassionate all special Ed. supporters. Women and children are safe. The so many officials that were also present are the guardian angel protecting the children. There are many offices out there that can help if you need them.

Don't be afraid. The offices of law enforcement and the board of education will continue to be on the front lines to fight any kind of violence against the innocents

Chapter 44

Naomi

Violent criminals don't hesitate to prey on girls like Naomi because all too often there is no reliable system in place to bring perpetrators to justice.

In fact, victims are often left vulnerable to retaliatory attacks for even daring to speak up. Even after the attack was over, Naomi and her mother were still in very real danger.

Bring young children out of the terror of sexual abuse.

Naomi is a daughter, a sister, and a girl with dreams. If you were lucky enough to know her, you knew someone who was ready to make the most of her gifts and passions.

That all changed during one terrifying night in her mother's home, when they found themselves in a waking nightmare. Naomi, then only 16 years old, heard a voice in the darkness.

"Wake up very slowly, don't scream, don't say anything. Do you see what this is?"

Naomi didn't know what was happening, but she did know one thing: Two men had broken into their home, and they were carrying a panga (machete).

Although they were there to rob Naomi's mother, the situation turned even more desperate as the two men raped Naomi. They threatened to kill Naomi and her mother if they went to the police.

Once the men left, Naomi's mother took her to the hospital. Word in their Kenyan village spread, and their community members urged them to seek help. Even with those threats of violence so fresh in their minds, they courageously shared their testimony with the police.

You can help give peace of mind to victims like Naomi.

In the wake of the attack, Naomi withdrew and grew silent. Her grades slipped. She would start a task, then her mind would fade away and she would "wake up" wondering what had happened. She would come to herself after long moments of being lost in her mind.

Even though her once talkative nature had been silenced, Naomi found the courage to use her voice.

While testifying in court, Naomi pulled on all her reserves of strength. "It was hard for me," she said. "It was very hard. Though I was trying to make myself like, 'I can do it. This is what they did to me, I can do it.'"

With IJM on her side, Naomi watched the case proceed in court. The family members of the accused would come at night, terrorizing them as they tried to sleep.

You can ensure women like Naomi don't have to live in fear.

Because of you, four years after the attack, Naomi finally saw justice when her attackers were sentenced to 15 years in prison.

We could not help survivors of sexual violence like Naomi without you. Your generosity meant that we could take on Naomi's case and connect her with an aftercare specialist who would help her get back to her bright, talkative self.

Today Naomi is safely living on her own. It was a long, difficult road to justice, but we're so thankful to have had you with us on this journey. Together we will continue to help others like Naomi.

Chapter 45

Attacked in her own Home

He came into her room while she was sleeping. He covered her mouth and she started to cry. Barbara recalled using broken sign language.

She was only 16 when she was hurt by her neighbor in her own home.

This wasn't the first time someone from her community took advantage of her weakness. She knew that it wouldn't be the last.

In an overloaded justice system, cases like Barbara's often fall through the cracks.

A young girl living in poverty with a hearing disability has almost no chance of being protected. The men that hurt her knew that and took advantage.

Barbara would see them often as she walked the narrow dirt paths of her small neighborhood. They gazed at her as she passed by, and though no words were exchanged their threats were loud and clear.

"Stay silent, or we'll make you pay".

Barbara's mother only knew that her little girl was being abused when they visited the doctor and found out Barbara was 15 weeks pregnant.

"I went cold," her mother said. "I couldn't wrap my head around it because, for me, she's my little girl."

Even though she had been intimidated, Barbara reported the criminals to local authorities. She had little reason to believe this would help; Less than 5% of all Sexual violence complaints end with a conviction, and there were 13,000 complaints that year alone. But hope compelled her to action.

When she bravely stood up for justice, you helped make sure she wouldn't stand alone. Thanks to people like you, Marie got the help she needed—help she wouldn't have received otherwise.

The first man was sentenced to 16 years and 5 months in prison, and the second received 25 years. Your intervention made it possible for IJM to walk with Marie through the legal process. You helped make sure she received critical care during the hardest part of the trial as she shared her testimony.

Part of the aftercare journey you helped provide ensures survivors are safer and less likely to be revictimized.

For Marie, it meant she could make her voice heard in more ways than one. She was given an opportunity to take sign language classes, empowering her to better communicate and continue speaking up for herself.

Today Marie and her family are safer because you allowed our team to stand by her, making sure she would never experience abuse at the hands of those men again.

Barbara has a story to tell, a story of resilience, bravery, and hope. Thank you for helping us tell her story.

Help more girls like Marie find safety

Chapter 46

The Beggers

Cathy grew up with her mother and three brothers in the housing projects in New York City.

Her mother worked hard as a janitor to provide for Cathy and give her a happy childhood. They were doing well.

Then, her father came back into their lives. The only thing that Cathy remembers about him was that one day he just took off with his mistress. Now, Cathy's childhood was over....

"He trapped us..." Cathy remembers.

At night, he would come home drunk and beat her mother. During the day, while her mother was at work, his attention shifted to Cathy and her brothers. He'd take them down to the street and force them to beg for money at the streetlights. This was exhausting and dangerous work for children.

Yet what he did in the dark was far worse for Cathy. During the night, Cathy's father would sneak into her bedroom and abuse her. Then he threatened to kill her family if she ever spoke up.

Sadly, many of the children living around the projects experienced a similar terror.

You can stop this form of violence against innocent children. How? It is very easy. Just trust your teachers.

In the ghettos, where many victims of this crime are abused by the ones closest to them, fear keeps these children from speaking up about their abuse or reporting it as a crime. So, Cathy suffered his repeated assaults in silence.

When her mother learned about his adventures, she took Cathy and her brothers out of the house and fled to the church.

After their escape, Cathy's mother reported the crime to the local authorities. Yet without the resources to hire a lawyer, there was little hope it would ever reach a verdict.

But guess what? The minute they entered the courtroom, everything changed. The Special Education team and the Police Department had worked together to help Cathy.

This is Cathy's story, an incredibly hard one that's all too common for many children in New York. Bear with us because you're about to find out how we, the teachers, changed everything…

We helped her process her hurt and shame by providing her with professional aftercare and counseling.

We gave her the strength to break the silence, testify against her father and secure an 8-year prison sentence.

Everyone deserves justice, no matter who you are or where you live.

Cathy went back to school and graduated high school. Nine years later, she now has a son and knows exactly what she wants to do with her life. She is studying at John Jay College to become a lawyer.

Chapter 47

—·◦~✦~◦·—

Betrayed By Her Father

For years, Bertha had been sexually and physically abused by her father. After she was placed in foster care, she harmed self. That is when got therapy and started taking antidepressants….

Some of her first memories, from when Bertha was 7, were hearing her mother and big sister Belinda complain about how she got too much attention from her dad. They called her "Daddy's little girl."

Bertha was happy to be loved by her whole family, but her father's love was the most precious.

Everything was going well for her when she was very young. School was fun and she loved going into the classroom in her uniform that her mother had ironed the night before.

Bertha had two best friends. They all had pink Barbie backpacks and saw themselves as beauty queens. They had high self-esteem. Some kids at school saw them as conceited.

After school her father would pick her up and take her to the "bodega", corner store. Her father would tell her to get whatever she wanted. If she couldn't go, he brings her Doritos, her favorite treat.

Around this time, my mother sat down with me and my sister and said, "We aren't your birth parents." I said, "No, Mommy!" because at first, I didn't understand what she meant.

She explained that our parents had died when Linda was 5 and I was 3, and that she and Daddy had adopted us the next day. They were friends of our birth parents. Linda had a few memories of our birth parents, but I don't have any.

It hurt to find this out, but I handled it well. My life was fine, and I felt happy with these parents, the only ones I remembered.

But everything changed one day when I was 10. I would never be that happy, trusting girl again.

I was home alone with my father that day, using the computer in the living room. I sensed someone behind me.

Slowly I stopped typing. I smelled my father's cologne, and then he was standing too close to me. I wondered what was going on. He whispered in my right ear, "Your ears are beautiful,' and then he licked my ear.

It felt like a dream; I touched the mouse to make sure this was real. "Is this happening to me?" I asked myself.

The second time he touched me, a few days later, I ran away afterwards and locked myself in the bathroom. He knocked on the door and slowly I opened it. He said in a pleading voice, "Please don't say anything to anyone, not even your mother." I wasn't sure what to do; I put my head down.

He kept touching me for three years, almost every day. It made me scared, sad, and angry. I was angry at the world and angry at God because it felt like He gave me something too hard to deal with.

I began to ask, "Why?" I felt like I was being punished by God but wasn't sure what I had done to deserve that.

The thought of going home from school and seeing my father disgusted me. I was also scared because I didn't know what he was going to do to me next.

Over the three years, the things he did got worse. I felt like I was in a different world and that I wasn't living my own life. I was living the life of someone else, a young girl who no one cared about who was getting abused by the man she called Dad or Papi.

I tried to make sense of what was happening. My father didn't seem to know if I realized what he was doing was wrong.

It felt like he considered this more of the same love he'd shared with me when I was a little kid. In my family, hitting a kid is part of loving a kid, and he seemed to think that sexual molestation was loving, too.

But even though I was confused, I was sure that this wasn't the love a father is supposed to give a daughter or the love, as a daughter, I had to accept.

I kept it all inside for three years and then I began keeping a diary to let it out. Soon after that, I told my sister.

She said my dad had on occasion molested her as well and how scared she'd been that he was going to do the same to me.

I asked her, "Is that why you kept on telling me not to wear shorts around Dad or show my skin?" She nodded her head yes, and we hugged each other and cried.

I began to feel angry that he had hurt her, too. I wanted my sister to always be OK like she had always wanted me to be OK. I loved her so much and knowing that he'd hurt us both made me want to fight.

I wanted to stop this from happening to us. But I still couldn't imagine telling my mother. She loved my father and did everything he said. She'd say, "He pays the bills."

Four days later, my secret spilled out again. It was the day of my parent-teacher conferences, and my mother, my sister, and I drove into school together in the evening.

When we got to my homeroom, my teacher started to tell my mother how I was doing with my assignments. My mother does not speak English well, and she got confused. She called my father, and he came in to translate what my teacher said.

But he was telling her the opposite of what my teacher was saying! When my teacher said, "Virgen is doing well," he'd translate, "Virgen is messing up." I got mad. "That's not what the teacher said!" I protested to my mother.

I knew my father was doing this to hurt me. He was mad at me because earlier in the day he wanted me to go sit with him inside the bodega with his friends.

Now that I was no longer a little kid, I hated doing this: It was embarrassing when someone I knew from school would walk in the bodega and see me sitting on a milk crate with a bunch of men listening to Spanish music and joking.

My father would stare at me every time he took a sip of his beer. I'd sit there watching the black cat that lived in the store wandering around, wishing I was home.

So earlier that day, I said, "No, I don't want to go to the bodega with you." He was angry and decided to get me in trouble with my mother by lying about what my teacher said. I was so angry at how he was acting at the parent-teacher conference and so sick of him.

I was also sick of feeling scared to fall asleep because I knew he'd come to the room, and I'd feel him breathing and smell his cologne before he started touching me. I was sick of his lies and of the way he treated people, especially his family.

That night, my mother went to hit me with the belt, and I started to cry. My father came into the room. My mother asked why I was crying so hard, and I told her, "Mommy, Father has been touching me in a wrong way."

For an instant I felt better for telling. Then I noticed that she didn't even look sad. She looked like she knew already but didn't care. My father yelled that I was lying.

I ran to my room and lay down on my bed crying. I hoped that I would wake up the next morning and this would all be a nightmare.

On Sunday, we went to church as usual. My mother spoke to me and my sister nicely, no yelling. She said, "We are going to go to church right now and pray.

What happened was that someone did witchcraft on your father. Someone probably put his picture upside down, someone who hates him. It was nothing but a witchcraft, so let's pray and then forget about it."

I felt confused and began to wonder, "Can that be true?" I knew that my mother wasn't the only one who believed in witchcraft, but did

I? I gave myself some time to think about what I believe in and what I thought was wrong and right.

I decided that my mother was wrong and that she didn't want to accept the truth. I was 13 and I was alone, against my parents.

Soon after that, a teacher found my diary: Looking back, I think I left it at school on purpose. Then ACS got involved. I was taken out of my home, but then begged to go back to be with my sister because she was very sick.

I stayed with my family another few months, and my father's abuse changed. It was less sexual and angrier and punishing.

Besides his smell, I was most afraid of his hands. He used them to feel underneath my shirt or hit me when I didn't do what he told me to do.

Each time I said "No" to him he would get mad and punish me. He acted like he owned me and like I had to do whatever he wanted me to.

ACS took me away from my parents for good soon after that. I have been in care ever since and have struggled to get free from what my father did.

His abuse, the secrecy, and my mother's denial broke my sense of self. I began to feel that I meant nothing if the father I'd loved so much could take advantage of me and not care.

One day I began cutting my left wrist, and I cut and cut and didn't stop cutting until I felt that I had done what everyone else was doing to me. I had started to believe that it was meant for me to feel pain.

Soon after I went into care, I made my first suicide attempt and got addicted to cutting.

I was diagnosed with major depressive disorder as well as P.T.S.D., post-traumatic stress disorder, and I still struggle with mood swings.

The doctors told me that all this was a direct effect of my father's abuse. I began to live a life of depression, of relying on antidepressants, of counting on a therapist to help me make it through my day.

All my cutting and suicide attempts may have been me trying to destroy that little girl who was abused by her father.

If I destroyed her, I thought, then what would be left was the younger girl, the one who could trust.

But that didn't work. The older girl was more lost than ever because she had escaped the abuse but didn't understand why she kept the pain.

My father's betrayal makes me wonder, "Am I important? Am I a person someone should take advantage of? Did my parents ever really love me and why did they stop?"

I feel like I'm only just starting to know who I am. Accepting what happened, saying "Yes, I was sexually abused," helps me find my identity.

I still have difficulties trusting guys. I hate to say it, but I feel like men are all the same. I feel that if my own father abused me, then anyone could. It's hard to trust anyone after you trusted someone completely and that person hurt you.

I am still working on my self-esteem. I want to accept that I am pretty and that my parents didn't mistreat me because I was ugly. I'm also trying to understand that I am important, that no one may take advantage of me like my father did.

I believe that everyone has his or her own path, where you sometimes face things, you don't want to.

On my path I've had to face what my father did to me. I know that many young teens face this, and I want them to know that they are not alone and should not give up.

It's hard to accept that the first guy who touched me was my father, and that the man who was supposed to protect me hurt me, and that the happy girl was turned into a sad girl and now an angry girl.

I have accepted it. I get myself back by moving forward with my life. By getting myself out of danger; by advocating for myself in foster care; by getting into college; by writing and painting and making friends; by still living, I realize that I am strong.

My father took away the happy girl who trusted everyone, but he didn't take all of me.

Chapter 48

Didn't Get To Be A Kid

My childhood was drug dealing, abuse, death, and chaos. I never got to "do kid things" and it's hard to trust people...

As a child, I wanted to do kid stuff and play with other kids. But instead, I was put into adult situations very young. My family home was a trap house, a place people come to buy drugs.

The drugs my mom sold out of our apartment in the Brooklyn included cocaine, weed, and different kinds of pills. I would also see people I didn't know go into my mom's and my sister Carla's room and then I'd hear the noises of them having sex. My mom prostituted herself and I think my sister did, too.

My oldest sibling, Felicita. She was 11 years older than me, and then my mom had Tanya, Tom, Anthony, and me, one after another.

We all had different dads. I didn't know my dad, but the man in the pictures looked like a future version of me. I knew he was one of Harlem's drug dealers. He didn't have much going for him.

He didn't go to school when he was younger, and he was either in prison or doing illegal things.

My sister Felicita was the only one who had a bond with her dad. When she was about 3, her dad got out of prison and started taking care of her. When she was 12, she went to live with her dad's side of the family to escape life at my mom's.

I knew way too much about adults' relationships. When I was 8, my favorite aunt came over to talk to my mom about her boyfriend sexually abusing her.

I overheard their conversation from the next room, and I understood that my aunt's boyfriend was choking and hitting her while they had sex. I knew what having sex was from television and movies and from hearing the noises from my mom's room. It seemed nasty and I didn't understand why people did it.

I knew what was happening to my aunt was worse. Right after my aunt's confession, my mom went out in the hallway of our building to sell her drugs.

I went into the kitchen and asked my aunt why she was sad. I wanted to show her I cared for her. I thought she needed a talk and some love. She said, "You're too young to understand," but gave me a big hug and cried on my shoulder.

After my mother and other family members took their Xanax and weed and whatever else, they'd tell me to go to my room and play with my toys or my video games.

I knew after they did the drugs, I'd be on my own for the night. I would eat and go to sleep while they argued and did other things loudly.

My brother and sisters were known in my hood as the next generation of drug dealers.

They were smarter than my mother but still stupid. They went to school and made some right decisions but still sold drugs for my mother and represented the Bloods in our hood.

My brothers got into fights and my sisters looked weird. Felicita had enough sense not to rep Blood or sell drugs.

She focused on school, especially after she moved in with her dad, who showed her the right path in life.

My mom went to prison for a street brawl with some of our neighbors when I was about 7. She was there for about six months, but she didn't learn anything.

When she came out, she continued to sell drugs and fight. She used to go out without feeding her kids. A lot of times during 1st and 2nd grade, I was so hungry I fell asleep in school.

The summer after 2nd grade, on the 4th of July, my mom's house got robbed. They stole jewelry and electronics and broke a lot of furniture, I guess to send a message.

I was moved to my grandparents' house. Right after I got there, my grandmother, who had cancer, went to the hospital for stomach pain. While I was visiting her, she started shaking and bumping, and spit came out of her mouth. I went to get doctors for help. The room was cold, and nothing seemed real. The doctors pronounced her dead.

At the time, I didn't feel mad or upset. I was just shocked. I replayed that day in my mind afterward. Sometimes when I was going to sleep, I would replay the image. I felt guilty that I hadn't been able to save her.

My grandpa became depressed after his wife died. Every day for about a week, he drank and smoked heavily, missing important appointments.

Two weeks after my grandmother died, he got robbed at gunpoint by a 17-year-old he owed money to. The teenager shot my grandpa in the chest for $1,280. He died a couple hours later.

I went to stay with my aunt because my mom's house was unsafe. My mom's drug customers had threatened to hurt me or kill me to get at her. What drug dealers did to people was another thing I wish I didn't know about as a 7-year-old.

Looking out the window, I would see and hear dealers fighting with people about money.

My aunt took care of me for the rest of the year. After my grandma's funeral I said my goodbyes to my mom and the rest of the family and went home with my aunt. At her house I clung to her, saying "I love you." I wanted to make her feel happy.

She was upset about her parents' deaths and about her boyfriend abusing her. I would hear him hurting her in the middle of the night. I don't know if my cousins knew because I pretended, I didn't know, and they never brought it up either.

Meanwhile, at school, I was being bullied. This was a lot to deal with at a young age. To escape my life, I watched basketball. My favorite team was the Knicks, and my favorite Knick was Carmelo Anthony.

On the court, he was a beast, and outside the court he was inspirational. He often said, "Never give up" in post-game interviews after a hard loss.

In my aunt's house, the tone was peaceful, comfortable, not ghetto. My cousins were nice to me. They shared their Xbox with me. We watched SpongeBob SquarePants together and created things with Magic Sand and Play-Doh.

My aunt was nice, too. She bought me ice cream after school and, if I was good all week, pizza from Dominos.

When I messed up, she talked to me about what I did wrong. One time I lied to her about breaking her phone charger. Instead of hitting me, she asked for an apology.

I would study with my cousins and play outside. They were close to my age, and we talked about our favorite movies and shows.

My aunt and cousins were nonviolent, while my family had abused me physically since I could walk and talk.

I wasn't as lonely at my aunt's. For the four months I was living there, I could forget about the other stuff I was put through at school and at my mom's.

By the beginning of 3rd grade, I was on top of my grades and happy with my life. The bullying had stopped. That October, I switched to a school closer to where my aunt lived. I liked that I didn't have to see the people who had bullied me. Switching schools gave me a chance to start over and be happier and more positive.

Still, even at my aunt's I was too close to adult situations. In the middle of the night, I'd hear yelling about money or unwanted sex.

I was too young to help her while I was there. My aunt went through a bunch of problems and later she told me she suffers from major depressive disorder.

She also has post-traumatic stress disorder, PTSD. She became pretty messed up, and I went back to my mom's. My aunt and I don't talk anymore.

The lack of a good role model had a lasting effect. When I was 14, I went into care after my mom cracked open my face with a skateboard.

After I went into care, I felt very alone and lost hope. I turned to drugs. Marijuana made me feel happy and laugh a lot. I sold drugs for a few months to get money, which helped fill the hole of loneliness.

I realized I could ruin my future if I stayed on that path. Now I look at drug dealers as weak, and I don't touch drugs. I want to stay in school and off the streets for the simple reason that I don't want to end up dead or in jail like everybody around me.

Seeing the messed-up lives of my grandma and grandfather, my mother, my siblings, and even my aunt makes me determined to have a good life.

I promised myself that I'd finish high school, get a job, and make enough money to support myself.

On the negative side, it's hard to trust people. To prevent bad situations, I stay humble and somewhat isolated. I don't push people out of my life, but I hold back.

I give enough love to make people love me but not enough love to where they can hate me. It's sort of like feeding a child: You want to give the child enough food to fill their tummy, but not so much that they're overstuffed and throw up.

I've seen love turn into hate quickly after a person has been let down, lied to, or when people just didn't turn out to be what the other imagined them to be.

To avoid those traps, I put into a relationship what I'd like to get out. I don't trust people yet, but the sort of person I would trust in the future would be kind, genuine, positive, and caring.

For now, I want to keep the painful things I've been through to myself. I'd like to forget about them and just move on. I want to try to be happy and do some of the things I couldn't do as a kid, like go to Disneyland and to a Knicks game.

People say everything happens for a reason. I didn't get to live life like a normal kid, and I wonder if that wasn't meant for me. I don't know now why I had to suffer so much, but maybe in 20 years I will understand it.

Chapter 49

A Year in the Dorm Project

E lena tried the New York City program the Dorm Project for a year. She experiences sexual harassment, verbal abuse, identity theft, and other affronts. She likes her tutor but not living in the dorm.

The Dorm Project is a three-year-old program that lets New York City foster youth stay in dorms year-round.

Before I moved into a dorm as part of the Dorm Project, in January of my sophomore year, I lived at home for a semester and a half while I went to LaGuardia Community College in Queens.

I had the opportunity to dorm at Queens College, an hour away from LaGuardia, and I took it.

I looked forward to the independence, relationships, and diverse experiences of living in a dorm. I appreciated that the Dorm Project offered tutors and College Success Coaches, CSC, to foster youth.

I met with my CSC every week to discuss personal and academic issues. Every foster youth in the Dorm Project gets a CSC to help keep us on the right track—mentally, emotionally, and physically.

I switched CSCs a couple of times, and my last one, Ashley, was very nice. I trusted her and her guidance.

I was placed with two young men in a suite. I shared a room with a girl, and the two boys shared a room on the other side of the suite. We all shared a kitchen and living room area.

From age 11 on, I grew up in kinship care with my grandmother, so I had never experienced group homes, residential treatment centers, RTCs, or even foster homes.

Perhaps if I had lived with other foster youth, I'd have been better prepared for the conflicts that followed.

I had trouble with all three of my suitemates. My female roommate would have her boyfriend spend the night without consulting me.

They'd have sex in the room while I waited somewhere else. My male suitemates often hosted two other guys I was uncomfortable with.

One of those visitors called me a "bitch"; another made crude remarks about my body.

My possessions weren't safe. My suitemates or their guests ate my food and stole a watch, a ring, a hat, and other possessions.

Someone in the suite opened a credit card under my name, and I'm still trying to get my credit cleared up.

I didn't want to snitch. I did tell my CSC about these things, but she felt more like a therapist than an authority figure. She couldn't do anything, as far as I could tell.

One of my male suitemates shoved me in the chest, and the other sexually harassed me. That's when I reached out to other CSCs and the director of the Dorm Project.

They all told me they were setting up a meeting about my complaints that would include staff from my agency, Queens College, and the Dorm Project.

I emailed various staff 19 times in the first weeks of July, but the meeting never took place. I also contacted someone from ACS in July. They told me there were no rooms available, so I couldn't just move out.

I felt like the CSCs didn't have enough control over the youth. I watched youth speak to CSCs any way they wanted and do whatever they wanted.

I reported all of it, but those who harmed me were not punished or stopped. Finally, after more than seven months of feeling scared, I was moved into my own room.

I dorm at Queens College for a year and graduated from LaGuardia with an associate degree. I transferred to SUNY New Paltz.

During the holidays, I went to my grandmother's. I lost the $930 monthly stipend from the Dorm Project and the awesome tutors and my CSC Ashley. What I gained was my mental health.

I wish the Dorm Project had disciplined the students more. Yes, every foster youth deserves a chance, but you can't put other youth in danger because of that.

Youth who were breaking the rules and harming other students weren't removed or, as far as I know, even disciplined.

Still, I had amazing tutors at the Dorm Project and eventually a CSC who I really liked. I keep in contact with my tutor, and he is helping me research graduate schools.

The New York Foundling declined to comment on Elena's story. They do not release student names of identifying information "as a matter of policy and privacy."

Chapter 50

I Want to be Adopted

My foster mother and I had conflicts over money in the pandemic, but I still want her as my forever family.

My parents abused and neglected me, and I went into care when I was 15. I lucked out getting Tere for a foster mother.

She was the first true mother figure I had. Six years later, I am still living with her, and she is in the process of adopting me.

I can talk to Tere for hours without feeling as if I'm being annoyed. Tere gives me advice about school, work, and girls. I tell her what's going on and how I'm feeling. She helps me try to fix the problem.

I didn't have any of this with my biological mother, so I wanted to keep that mother-son relationship for as long as I could before I got my own place.

Right after I turned 19, my foster care agency tried to push me into a supportive housing apartment.

Supportive housing is different from public housing, which is run by the New York City Housing Authority or NYCHA. There is a lot more supervision and more rules in supportive housing. I had been on the list for a NYCHA apartment since I was 17, because a lot of low-income people need those apartments and were ahead of me on line.

I told my worker Donna that I wasn't ready for supportive housing. She asked, "Why not?"

I responded, "Umm, I don't have a job, or much money saved up."

She said, "You know, there is public assistance."

"I know, but I'm not trying to rely on the government for money." I felt like I was being forced to go on welfare, even though, if I had time, I could save up the money. I didn't want to be another Black person on public assistance.

At 19, I had already held a lot of jobs, but didn't know how to get loans and build credit. Tere was teaching me about credit and how to spot financial fraud.

I wanted more time to bond with Tere. Our connection helped me in a lot of ways. She showed me the value of hard work and dedication and how to keep up a household.

I told Tere that I'd been offered an apartment but wanted to stay longer with her. She said, "Of course. You're not ready to live on your own, financially, or emotionally." I was happy that she agreed and that she wasn't going to kick me out.

So, when Donna told me about the supportive housing apartment, I told her I wasn't ready, and I stayed with Tere.

Over the next several years, I got more prepared to live on my own. When the pandemic hit, I was working at my foster care agency as a youth advocate, a job I'd started in December 2018.

I helped foster youth connect to resources and took them on trips and gave them advice. I loved helping them change their life for the better. I was paid $15 an hour and worked 20 hours a week.

I had a second job driving for a car service. That paid between $500 and $850 a week.

In the middle of March 2020, my supervisor at the foster care agency told me not to come into work because of COVID-19.

I was disappointed, but I hoped the driving job would keep me from running out of money. Before the pandemic, I was able to save about half of what I made from the two jobs.

In the spring of 2020, when so many New Yorkers were getting sick and dying, earnings from my driving job dropped to about $175 a week.

I couldn't get the $1,200 stimulus payment because I didn't file taxes for 2018 or 2019. I tried but couldn't get approved for unemployment. I started to panic.

I started cleaning people's houses for $150; I got those jobs through some of my biological relatives and their friends.

I turned 21 in April, but stayed in care thanks to an extension often granted to youth who don't have a place to move to when they age out. I was still on the NYCHA list.

In June 2020, I asked Tere if I could get an allowance of $100 a month so that I could pay my phone bill. Under the extension, I knew she was still getting a check from foster care for me. She also gets checks for two other foster youth who live with us.

Tere said angrily, "I can't afford to hand out money right now due to the pandemic."

I responded with an attitude. "You got a stimulus check for you, plus $500 per child. Which means you got $1,500 extra."

Tere said, "You don't know what I got."

"Whatever," I said, and slammed my door.

Tere usually made me feel like a real son and I'm glad she's adopting me. But during the pandemic, she wouldn't give me money that I needed. I knew she had just gone on a shopping spree with her biological son when she said, "I can't afford to hand out money now."

It was hard to ask for help, and it hurt that she didn't want to. It made me feel like she wasn't really my mom. I felt like a mom should ask, "How can I help you get through this hard time?"

She owed me because I'm still officially in care. I didn't say anything to my agency because I don't want to get her in trouble.

I still want to be adopted because I want to be legally a part of Tere's family even if she can't support me financially.

At the same time, I have always known I want my own apartment after I turn 21. I want my own space, where it's quiet and clean and I can decorate the house how I want. I want to paint some of my walls red. I want to have parties and to bring girls home.

When I first applied to NYCHA, I did the three workshops that were supposed to give you a jump on the list. I maintained a clean legal record, held many jobs, and got all the physical exams they asked for.

I have no idea why I was on the list for almost four years. I have seen other foster youth get NYCHA apartments much faster.

In June, a few months after my birthday, my worker emailed me asking if I had checked my status on NYCHA. I told her, "Yes, I'm still on the waiting list."

She said "Bryant, you're 21 now, so we're in a rush to find you housing or to finalize your adoption."

I told her, "I want to be adopted and I want housing." The agency will pay the adoption costs now, but after a certain amount of time, they won't, she said. But during the pandemic, the courts were closed, so the adoption process had stopped.

I wondered if getting adopted was why I wasn't getting a NYCHA apartment. When I got on the list for public housing, my official goal was APPLA, which stands for Another Planned Permanent Living Arrangement.

That means the plan was for me to age out on my own, without a family. Someone at ACS told me that if my goal was APPLA when I first submitted my NYCHA application, that getting adopted after that wouldn't bump me out of line.

So, I'm not sure why my worker said that or why it was taking so long.

Then, in early February 2021, almost four years after getting on the list, I got the call! A NYCHA apartment was available in the borough of my choice, the Bronx.

You only get shown two apartments, so I will say Yes to the Bronx apartment unless it is falling apart. I took a building maintenance course, so I'm better than most people my age at fixing things up. I know how to put-up drywall and how to patch holes in walls. I have friends who do plumbing and electrical work.

Getting an apartment is a huge relief. I feel like I can step into my adult life now. I will file taxes for 2020, and hopefully I'll be able to get any stimulus checks the government sends in 2021.

When the pandemic ends, I'll pick the adoption process back up. I haven't spoken with my birth parents in months. They have never helped me, and they lost their parental rights years ago.

Yet I know they wouldn't like to hear Tere was adopting me. My biological mom would accuse me of "turning on family." So, I'm not going to tell her about the adoption.

Getting the apartment has made my relationship with Tere better. She seems happy for me. She said she will help me buy things for my house, and that she still wants me to come over for all holidays.

She also said, "I will still adopt you if you still want me to."

I told her I did. It means a lot to me to be Tere's legal child and to have a stable family.

It will help to feel supported as I set up my first household. There are legal as well as emotional benefits: In a medical emergency, Tere will be able to make decisions about my care.

Knowing that Tere has my back makes me feel confident going into the real world. I like knowing I can call her and say, "Mom I got this job done" or "Mom, I met this woman and I want you to meet her," or even, "Mom, I'm going through hard times, and I need some advice." I look forward to being a grown

Chapter 51

With A Father

Through my grief, I find he still lives on in my memory.'....

The day my dad got sick; I was out shopping with my mom. She bought me a little teddy bear. I was so excited to show it to him that I ran inside his bodega as fast as I could when my mom parked the car out front.

But when I got inside, he wasn't there. A coworker said he'd been rushed to the hospital. My dad had diabetes, but since I was only 7 years old, I didn't understand the seriousness of his illness. My mom just told me he was sick and would be better soon.

A few weeks later, my grandma picked me up from school. I was happy because she bought me a snow cone from the ice cream truck until it dropped on the ground.

I started crying since she wouldn't buy me another one. I had a fit that continued all the way up five flights of my building's stairs and I refused to go inside my apartment.

It wasn't until my mom came out with red eyes and wet cheeks that I realized something had happened that was bigger than my little problem. "I'm sorry, Natalie, I thought your father was getting better. But he's gotten worse."

When my mom took me to the hospital, I wasn't allowed upstairs to see him because I was too young. He died before I was able to see him one last time.

On the day of my dad's funeral, I didn't understand why everyone was staring at me with a pitiful look. And why was everyone so sad? I kept thinking I was going to finally get to see him. I didn't yet fully comprehend what death meant.

So much felt confusing to me. Before the service, I didn't understand why I was being introduced to relatives I'd never met before.

Why was he in a casket and not moving, and why did he look plastic and feel cold? When I saw him, I got scared and upset. I ran out of the funeral home crying, "I want to go home!"

What Is Death?

My cousins agreed to take me home during the funeral service. As we walked, they gave me hugs and kisses, telling me the same thing everyone else did: That he was in a better place where he wouldn't suffer and would feel peace, like he was taking a long nap.

They said he was in heaven and watching over me. He was my own personal guardian angel.

It made me feel better that he was still with me in spirit, but I would have preferred for him to be there with me. I wondered if he was taking a nap, why didn't he wake up? And how is he in a better place if I'm not with him?

Later that night, my mom took me back to the funeral home. My grandma asked a man who worked there to give the two of us time alone with my dad.

My mom cried and showed me a pillow under his head that she had made for him. We got down on our knees to pray together and say "I love you" one last time. She kissed his forehead, and helped me reach it so I could, too.

After his funeral his body was sent to Puerto Rico, to be buried with his relatives. I couldn't go, even though I wanted to.

After my dad died, my family talked about him in hushed tones or in Spanish so I couldn't understand them.

They didn't want to make me sad. But I didn't mind being sad and hearing them talk about him.

I thought then, and still do, that it's nice to learn things about my father that I didn't know before. Even after his death, he lives on in other people's memories, not just mine.

I missed him terribly. I couldn't run into his arms or hang out in his store anymore. Even though my parents were divorced, my dad and I were still close, and I would go to the bodega almost every day after school.

It had dingy turquoise floor tiles with a few missing, and a little deli counter. Behind the counter he usually put up my artwork, like a wooden picture frame I made with little shells around the edge.

The frame held a picture of us outside in the snow. He was kissing my cheek. When my dad had customers, I'd help count the money and give him the right amount of change.

That's how he helped me practice my math. Customers thought this was adorable. After he died, the bodega was left to my stepmother. Soon after though, they closed the store and a guitar store opened in that location.

Since we no longer had my father's financial support, my mom had to work longer hours at her office job.

My grandma would watch me on days that my mom worked, and I didn't have my after-school program.

One time I got dressed up in my grandma's clothes. I took one of her jackets and put on her scarf the way she did, with my pajama pants, a pink wig, and a pair of her heels.

I put on a fashion show for her, and she loved it, laughing and applauding. She couldn't take my dad's place, but it made me feel good anyway to have her attention and support while I was grieving him.

When my mom came home from work at night, I clung to her because I was afraid to lose her, too.

Even now that I'm older, I try not to say or do something that might jeopardize our relationship, whether it's failing a class, not doing what she tells me to, or even talking back.

If something happened to her, I would feel awful if our last interaction had been upsetting.

As I made my way through elementary school, I still had clear memories of my dad, but I became less sad.

Although his death was something my mom tried to explain to me, it was a concept that was too difficult for me to comprehend.

So, I pushed it to the back of my mind. "You'll understand when you're older," my mom and other relatives would say.

It wasn't until middle school, after he'd been gone for five years, that my bubble of ignorance popped, and I fully understood that he was gone forever.

I also learned that my dad didn't have to die so young: His death was caused by complications from diabetes and high blood pressure.

Though these are conditions that need to be treated, he kept saying he felt fine and wouldn't go to the doctor even though my mom often warned him about the consequences.

He just disregarded what she said, something a lot of my relatives do. It upsets me that his death could have been prevented if only he'd listened to my mom and gone to the doctor sooner.

Also, during middle school, I was bullied for not having a dad. One kid said, "Why don't you kill yourself, so you can be dead like your dad?"

It hurts to see girls doing things with their dads that I'll never be able to experience. When I graduated middle school, I missed not having him around to tell me how proud he was and how much he loved me.

This year, I didn't want to have Sweet 16 because I knew if I did, I couldn't do the father-daughter dance, or have him put high heels on my feet, like in Cinderella.

He will never be able to walk me down the aisle on my wedding day and tell me how beautiful I look. He'll never be able to scare away my boyfriends, and I'll never be able to get mad at him because he's embarrassing me.

Chapter 52

Violence Is Not Discipline

They look back on her mother's abuse and her own fighting at school. She is placed with her grandmother at age 11, goes to therapy, and learns to handle her own feelings.

Growing up, it was just my mom, my little sister Shania, and me in an apartment in Flatbush, Brooklyn. Watching my sister was my job. While my mom was cooking, at the store, or on the phone, I was supposed to keep Shania quiet and still. My mother often complained about our noise.

I tried my best not to upset my mom, but a lot set her off. She disliked when I called her "Mom," "Mommy," or "Mother." She'd say, "Can you stop? That is annoying," or, "Stop calling me that shit."

When I wanted to speak to her, I tapped her or went in front of her to get her attention. I started my sentences with "So," or, "Excuse me."

I wanted her to hug me, kiss me on the cheek, and tell me to have a good day at school like the other mothers did. I longed for a normal mother-daughter relationship.

Instead, she hit me with whatever was within reach shampoo bottle, hairbrush, or a toy. She'd hit me if school called her about my misbehaving, if I couldn't keep my head straight while she was doing my hair, or if I dropped a new shirt on the floor.

She hit my sister, too, but not as much. She hit me more perhaps because I was the oldest, so she considered me responsible for whatever my little sister had done.

I often went to school with bruises and marks on my body. My mother told me, "If anybody at school asks what happened tell them that Shania hit you with a toy. That's it." I did as I was told.

My gym teacher was the only one who noticed, and she often asked me if I was OK. I told her what my mom told me to say, and she always asked, "Are you sure?"

I know now that I was not OK at all. I was in constant fear at home, and at school, I did what I was taught at home. In the 2nd grade I was suspended twice for violence against others.

I thought I did it because I wanted to, but looking back, it was because of the effect my mother had on me.

I learned to hit or cause pain to people who upset me. I didn't know how else to express my discomfort.

My dad was unstable. He couldn't keep a job or an apartment, but I still loved him. He would come by occasionally and that's when we'd spend time together. I spent weekends at his mother's.

I loved it when my grandma picked me up on Fridays. She would hug and kiss me on the cheek. She also worried about me: My grandmother, aunt, uncles, cousin, and dad all saw the marks and bruises on my body. Even when I defended my mom and told them the story about Shania hitting me, my family knew it was her.

My grandma said once, "Nina, you need to stop hitting the poor girl. This has been going on for too long. You need to find another way to discipline her." But no one threatened to do anything because they thought my mother would stop.

The beating that changed all our lives came because my little sister spilled juice on our new bedroom curtains. I was 11 and Shania was 5. I didn't see her spill it, and I couldn't even see it on the curtain, but my mother could spot anything that wasn't right.

When she saw the stain on the curtains she backhanded me in the face, grabbed me by my hair and threw me into the radiator. I scraped my knee. She also threw a sneaker hard at my face. I cried to myself to sleep.

When I woke up the next day, I saw my banged-up knee and thought, "Not so bad. No heavy marks."

I brushed my teeth and did my hair without looking in the mirror. As I left for school, my mother grimaced, looking at my face and reminded me of the Shania excuse. I wondered why she looked so worried.

Then I got to my elementary school, and everyone there looked at me like they'd seen an alien.

I ran into the school bathroom and looked in the mirror. I was mortified: On my face was a vivid red outline of the bottom of the sneaker, as if stamped on me. It looked horrible.

I went to a couple of classes trying to be calm. Then I was called to the assistant principal's (AP) office. I sat down with my heart thumping.

The AP stared at me intently.

"How are you?"

"I'm fine."

"How is it at home?"

"Life at home is pretty OK."

"Can I ask you what happened to your face?"

"Oh yeah. Well, I was playing with my little sister, and she threw a toy at me."

The AP smiled. "Are you sure that's all that happened? You can tell me anything you want. It's going to be OK."

I wanted to believe her, but I didn't. I knew my mom would get in trouble and I was scared she was going to take it out on me. I stuck to my excuse, and she sent me back to class. I went home and 30 minutes later, there was a banging on the door. My mother and I were in the kitchen, my sister in our bedroom. My mom looked angry about the loud knocks.

She opened the door, and two men dressed like agents asked if she was Nina. She glanced at me before saying "Yes," and they said, "Come with us."

I Panicked; I called my sister out of the room wondering if this had to do with my meeting with the AP. The three of us went outside and got into a van parked in front. The entire mysterious ride, my mother glared at me. That glare was frightening.

As soon as we reached a place that looked like a day care, officers whisked my mother out of sight. Shania and I were taken to a room to speak to Kevin, a detective. This was all happening too fast; I left the room to look for my mom and saw a man putting her arms behind her back.

I suddenly felt numb. I went back to the room and sat next to my sister. Kevin started to ask questions.

"So, your mom hits you and your sister?"

"Yes, when she felt it was necessary."

"I see. So, when was it necessary?"

"Um, when I was misbehaving in school or wore something dirty by accident?"

I was trying to minimize the abuse, but my sister said, "Yeah, she hits us real bad! She does it all the time!"

After the interview, my sister and I got back in the van and strangers gave us hot pink Tommy Hilfiger backpacks with clothes and toiletries in them. The folks in the van conversed with us and made us feel comfortable and then drove us to my grandma's house.

Shania went back to my mother's a few months after we were taken from her. I have been at my grandmother's ever since, for seven years. Whenever I went to court, I would say that I wanted to stay there.

I missed my sister, but at my grandmother's I felt free. I didn't have to watch what I was doing in fear of being hit. It was a real home filled with care and sincerity. If I got in trouble at school my grandma would talk to me instead of abusing me physically and verbally.

It wasn't that easy for me to get rid of my bad ways, though. I was still getting in trouble a lot for being too talkative, disruptive, and "a nuisance." I told my grandmother I couldn't stop and that I wanted to kill myself. I felt as if the world hated me.

That's when I went to therapy at my foster care agency. I explained to my therapist it would just be easier if I was dead because I was a problem child to my grandmother, who didn't deserve that trouble.

I was grateful to live with my grandmother, so where was this behavior coming from? I wanted to be good; I just didn't know how. The therapist and I figured out that my mother's lack of love decreased my self-esteem.

As I got older, it got easier to control my behavior. I was more aware of why I did the things I did, and I changed. Once I got to high school, I was careful and pushed myself to make my family happy.

It was still difficult transitioning into being a non-violent person. When I felt like hitting I couldn't, so I took deep breaths and tried to be calm.

I did extracurricular activities and joined clubs. These kept me busy and made me happy; it was a fresh new start.

I stopped being afraid to stand up to my mother. After I moved out, I would visit every other weekend if I wasn't busy. She stopped hitting me, but she hasn't changed her ways. She had three more children after I moved out, and she beats them and Shania.

It's hard to see my little siblings go through what I went through. My mother has a bad temper; plus, some people from her West Indian culture believe discipline must involve pain. She had to go to classes for her anger, but they didn't work. Because she doesn't believe hitting kids is wrong, she didn't want to or try to stop.

Even though my mom is still abusive, I wouldn't call Children's Protective Services, CPS, on her because I'm afraid my siblings could be worse off in care, maybe separated. I do try to defend them when we're all together.

Recently, we all went to the beach with some friends of my mom's. The little kids were throwing sand at one another.

My mother yelled at my five-year-old brother, "Didn't I tell you to stay away from the sand?!" I remembered being in his shoes, hearing the yelling, waiting for the hits to come.

My mom's friend told her to relax. Annoyed but also a little scared, I yelled, "They're just kids! And it's a beach, you're going to get sand on yourself! You always act like little things are the end of the world!"

She quietly said, "I wasn't talking to you."

Love, Not Fear

It felt good to stand up to my mother. I wanted to open her eyes to how insensitive she was being. Even more, I wanted to show the little kids that it wasn't normal to be scared by Mommy. That Mommy was wrong.

My mother hasn't changed, but I have. Over the course of my four years in high school, I went from a problem child to a teenager slowly learning about herself and working on her issues. I just started college this fall.

I now get to do things for my siblings I couldn't before. I stand up for them, buy them things they need, and embrace them with love. I found the love I craved and needed from my grandmother, and I'm better able to show love now.

I know my mother was hit as a child and that she considered beating normal parenting. I know others from her culture agree.

The beatings did discipline me, but they messed me up inside as a child. If I never left her home, I'm not sure I would be the young woman I am today. I am lucky that I got to experience a loving home at my grandmother's.

What turned me from a violent, scared problem child into a happy, successful, loving college student was not beatings and fear; it was kisses and hugs, therapy, and self-knowledge. Finding out who you are is difficult when you suffered a loveless childhood. Abuse is hard to recover from, but it is possible.

Chapter 53

Not Safe Enough

Olivia is physically abused by her father as a young girl and begins to dissociate when she remembers it. She recognizes what she's doing and takes steps to stay present.

When I was very little, my father, Troy, beat me, but not my older sister or my mother. He chose me because he didn't think I was his child. He'd scream, "You're not mine; you're too light-skinned!" He did abuse my mother in other ways, though: He would yell degrading things at her and keep her from protecting me when he went off on me. These are some of my earliest memories.

Though the beatings hurt a lot, I learned not to show emotion. In my head, I would stray from the reality of my father pounding on my back while I clung to his leg, by thinking of happy thoughts and fairytale places. These imaginations were my "temporary relief."

When I was 4, my mother took me and my sister to a shelter in Spanish Harlem in New York. We never went back. It was great to be away from Troy; I felt safe for the first time in my life.

The shelter had free therapy. In therapy, when I talked about the abuse, I would start to relive it and feel it. To stop myself from crying, my mind would take me somewhere else. In the therapist's office, I daydreamed of my sister, my mother, and me secluded in an all-white room. That's when I first realized that memories could be so powerful and that I sometimes needed to get away from them.

Until therapy in the shelter, I had never talked about my father's abuse with anyone, not even my mother or sister or grandmother. When we sneaked away, my mother only said, "We are going to have to leave your father for a while." She never mentioned Troy or what had happened again.

I never second-guessed my family's "avoid-it" system; I would just go with the flow, because I didn't know what was going on. I trusted my mother and her judgment. My family never talked about feelings.

To finally talk about the abuse in therapy felt like facing the things my family never discussed. Even though I didn't want to feel anything, I did anyway; I felt overwhelmed and alone with my heartbreak. When it got too bad, I'd go to my daydreams.

In therapy I asked myself, "Olivia, why did this happen to you? What did you do to deserve this? What could you have done differently?" My therapist always reassured me that the abuse wasn't my fault, but I didn't believe her. I worried that we left home only for my benefit because Troy focused his abuse on me.

We got away from Troy, but then my mother started drinking a lot. I would come home from school and find her dizzy.

I learned to pray by speaking out loud in my room. I'd say, "Dear Lord, I need your blessings and guidance." I started to incorporate Him into my talks to myself about my life, my past, Troy, and my mother.

That's how I learned to speak my feelings. Because with Him there was no judgment. I began to tell the Lord things that I had been scared to admit to myself. I could tell Him about sins I had committed and sins that I wanted to commit. I tell Him everything.

During prayer, I learn things that I didn't even know about myself, like my creativity and my likes and dislikes. It all starts pouring out of my heart; I don't stop myself from saying anything (if I curse, I apologize).

Feelings I've pushed away come out when I pray—sort of like the tape, but good. It's another mind compartment, but in this compartment, I can feel and discover things about myself.

And that is how I began to know myself. Doing that was extremely difficult, because I kept it in for so many years. It was also difficult to pray because I had to learn not to lie to myself and to admit the truth.

Whenever I pray, I start to understand what's bothering me. Often, I cry. I feel overwhelmed by sadness about the things that have happened to me.

The Uses of Dissociation

There's still a lot of pain to avoid. I still live at home with my mother who continues to drink. She tells me that I'm the reason she drinks. When she says this, I just walk away, because I don't want to feel it. I don't think it's true, but it hurts. If I could feel more now, that might make me cry.

My best friend is in foster care, and her situation scares me. As bad as it is with my mother, I'm not ready to risk making my life worse by calling ACS and going into care. Plus, I don't want to get my 3-year-old brother taken away from his mother. So, I am stuck.

If I had complete control of my life, I would let myself feel emotions. The only way you can gain experience in life is by going through the pain, even though emotions can feel like they are getting "out of control."

But I'm not safe enough to do that yet. My life has been controlled by people who have hurt me since the day I was born. Most 15-year-olds have parents who have their best interests at heart, but I don't. I'm on my own except for God.

I want to be able to take my life back. Praying is giving me back some of my feelings. I like having my feelings because I want to be honest with myself and others. I will never learn to deal with problems if I'm not mentally present for them. I don't want to keep dissociating because it's a safety blanket, a fantasy, and I'd rather live the truth.

Chapter 54

Only Lies

One Sunday afternoon, after a very tiring morning, my Aunt Emma, my cousin Luis, and I sat on the couch watching TV. We enjoyed a movie and a few shows, but the programming was interrupted by frequent advertisements.

There was one ad that caught my attention: a woman dressed in black, walking seductively through a humongous house. She was moving amongst costly diamonds, pearls, and other rare jewels, posing, and standing in different ways that might seem appealing to viewers.

Not one word was uttered in the advertisement; there was just a little music coming from what sounded like a violin.

None of us had a clue what the advertisement was for, so we all gave our opinions. I said that it must be for jewelry. My cousin said maybe it's a perfume, and my aunt said it might be for an expensive watch.

Suddenly, at the end of the ad, a picture of a car and its name came up. All of us were wrong: This was a car commercial.

I started asking myself, "What did the whole portrayal of the woman with the seductive look, the humongous house, and all the jewelry have to do with the car?" I didn't see the link between the images and the product being promoted.

I continued asking myself what all those different scenes said about the value of the car, but it seemed that the answer was: nothing. I wanted to make sure it wasn't just me who was missing something, so I asked my cousin what she thought about the advertisement. "It was captivating," she said, "but I would never have figured out what it was for."

From that moment on, I started observing different advertisements closely to see if they conveyed useful messages to their viewers. I noticed that most didn't, and quite a few were misleading.

For example, there was one ad with a man drinking expensive wine, and he gets attention from women. The ad seemed to suggest that the attention came because he was drinking this wine.

I think most people recognize drinking a certain brand of alcohol does not literally get anyone attention from the opposite sex.

However, ads like this do subconsciously influence people. By presenting attractive or captivating images, advertisements get viewers' attention; then, advertisers hope that viewers will associate whatever happiness and pleasure they see in those ads with the product being sold.

The ads never explain what exactly the benefits of their products are, because the actual benefits will always be less appealing than the idea of a whole lifestyle full of exquisite moments and total success.

The advertisers hope that viewers won't question the real-life benefits of their products. They would prefer that viewer be seduced by the dreamlike images and simply desire what they see.

If you fall into this trap, these ads can heavily influence your decision-making. They can lead you to buy things you don't need, or even behave in ways you wouldn't otherwise.

For example, a car ad that portrays a young man racing along a road with blue sky and perfect surroundings might inspire young men to buy this car; it also might cause them to speed and cause accidents.

In fact, the most attractive part of the ad may be the clear sky and beautiful landscape, which you can't buy or get through your actions.

So, people are chasing something unattainable when they are influenced by these ads.

Thinking about this makes me feel sorry for consumers. They buy into ads that have little to do with the actual products they are selling. When this happens, disappointment is inevitable.

I remember once, when I was very young, I cried uncontrollably for an expensive doll that I saw on TV.

She looked awesome and was able to sing, dance, and sit up. She had various types of clothing and sparkled on the screen. I was determined to get her and so cried my heart out until my parents bought her for me.

But to my surprise, she was not as beautiful and strong as she looked in the ad. She didn't dance as well, and her shoes didn't fit as well as they did on TV. I only had her for a few weeks before I grew tired of her.

Adults are bound to be just as unhappy with the things they crave based on advertising. Companies convince people to purchase things for no reasonable purpose at all.

I believe that individuals should have their eyes open about the products they see in ads. We should recognize the difference between things we need and things we want because we have been manipulated to want them.

We should see that buying too many products will only make us dissatisfied and might even hurt our financial stability and keep us from saving money.

It's human to be a little unsatisfied, and advertisements have taken that weakness as an opportunity to make people believe that they should purchase certain products to achieve happiness.

So next time you feel the urge to buy something you see in an ad, stop for a minute, and ask yourself, "Do I really need those dresses, cars, or shoes?"

Chapter 55

A Friendship Ends

Millie and I were in the same religion class and freshman year of high school….

At first, she gave me dirty looks or rolled her eyes when we made eye contact. I had no idea why.

One day, however, she complimented me in class. Surprised, I told her I thought she was pretty, and we exchanged phone numbers.

Next thing I knew, we were best of friends. I asked her later, "Hey, why did you give me so many dirty looks before?" She said it was because she thought I hung out with the cool, troubled crew from our school.

We texted every day and hung out after school. Freshman year flew by, and by the time we were sophomores, our conversations became deeper and more personal.

Her dad died just as we were getting close. I had never met him, but I went to his funeral.

As Millie shared her loss, I opened about having been abused by my mother and going into kinship care with my grandmother when I was 11.

I appreciated how she handled her loss. I didn't realize at first how she had been affected by her father's death because she seemed so strong. She kept going. She wasn't a quitter. I hoped to handle my own troubles with similar calm.

Knowing how much we each had suffered, we boosted each other up. I'd remind her what a good singer and dancer she was, and she'd tell me I was a great speaker and performer.

Madison didn't allow me to carry any baggage alone; she made sure I spoke about whatever I was feeling or going through. She always knew when something was wrong.

No one else knew that we were down on ourselves. People assumed we were fine because we were "conventionally attractive" and because we were always laughing together.

We were going on 16 and both had therapists who didn't do much for us. We began smoking weed together, and Madison began drinking. We enjoyed getting high, but as with everything else, we came to the same conclusion around the same time.

We met in the girl's bathroom in school one afternoon after smoking together. Madison said, "Bro, I don't like doing this sometimes. I hate the feeling of having to sit and deal with the high until it goes away."

"I feel the same way. It doesn't solve anything; it just traps me in a different state of mind that I can't escape from. I just want to be sober after a while. Weed can really mess you up sometimes."

"That's exactly how I feel."

"We don't need it. Let's just stop for a while."

After that, we helped each other fight the temptation to smoke or drink to escape. We were so similar in our intellectual and emotional intelligence and self-awareness. Having such a reflective and intuitive friend helped me realize how smart I was.

We were on the speech forensics team together. Speech forensics is an oral interpretation of literature pieces. We read prose and poetry in front of judges.

When Madison and I competed against each other, she usually won. But when we were in different categories, it would be easier for me to win. I was jealous, but I tried not to let it come between us.

Meanwhile, she was jealous of my relationships with boys. She said that she had never had a relationship with anyone. When I pointed out that none of my relationships lasted, she said, "At least you had them."

But even expressing jealousy helped us see each other's strengths. We were so intensely bonded, it felt like we were the same person. Usually the word "soulmate" is used for romantic relationships. But if a soulmate is a person ideally suited to another, Madison was mine.

Different Colleges, Drifting Apart

When we went to colleges in different boroughs of New York, we continued to meet up and text each other. But after freshman year, Madison became less available. I reached out to her and got upset when I didn't get an immediate response. So, I called her less and less.

When she transferred to University of the Arts in Philadelphia for sophomore year, she began posting on Twitter things I expected her to only tell me—like about her new boyfriend.

I saw her distancing herself from me without communicating that she needed space, the way she would have back when we told each other everything.

I wondered if she'd forgotten all about me and created a new life. The intensity of my emotions about our friendship made me feel foolish considering her pulling away.

I decided to let her go instead of communicating how I felt. There didn't need to be a conversation if her actions were telling me everything I needed to know, I thought. It hurt like hell.

I suffered every day from not talking to her but refused to put my pride aside.But then a few months later, I sent her a hurt and angry text: "It seems like you're doing what you want to do, Madison, so I think you should continue doing that."

She replied, "Lol ok Ericka, I'm going to continue doing me." Madison said I was acting like an obsessive boyfriend.

I knew I needed to depend on her less, but it was hard to let go. We'd gone from telling each other everything for five years, to telling each other nothing. Lacking a solid relationship with my own mother, I depended on Madison for a lot.

I never got so emotionally open with or close to a boyfriend or anyone else as I did to Madison. I knew it was over when she came to New York from Philly several times without even telling me.

I only learned about her visits from social media. The relationship was out of my control, and it hurt so much. I turned to casual sex for comfort. I felt numb. I lost myself.

Lessons From the Suffering

After a year and a half, I began to bounce back from that bleak phase. I started realizing that I didn't know who I was anymore when I hooked up with guys I didn't care about.

I didn't have many friends because I compared everyone to Madison, and nobody measured up to her. I had put her on a pedestal.

I realized that I was mourning her. Some friends assured me that we would eventually talk again, and I hated hearing that. It felt like false hope.

I had a new therapist, and I told her about my heartbreak and how I'd then numbed myself with self-destructive behavior. I realized in therapy that I had suppressed the loss of my friendship with Madison and had lost my sense of self. In high school we told each other every thought. Without that intense communication, I wasn't sure who I was anymore. My behavior forced me to see who I was becoming.

With the help of my therapist, I realized I had to do alone what we had done together, and to take what I'd learned and move forward.

We shared so much that she gave me the gift of self-examination. With Madison, I went deeper into my insecurities and my sadness than ever before.

I can keep that gift and know myself and honor my feelings without her. I continue to be an open book and a genuine person, and that's largely because I felt so seen and valued by her.

Madison also taught me a painful lesson: Just because I give doesn't mean I will always receive, and I can't expect reciprocation from everyone.

I was kind to her, and she was with me. I will continue to be kind with others because it is the right thing to do, even if I don't get the appreciation, I got from her.

Being true to myself is my top priority now. Some people in my life will appreciate me; others may not, and I can't control that.

I can just focus on those who do see me. I take pride in who I am, the impact I've had on others, and what I've accomplished in my life so far.

I know myself intimately now, thanks both to Madison's friendship and thanks to the pain I suffered when it ended. I will never be loved, understood, and accepted fully for who I am by anyone, even though it did feel like that for a few years with Madison. But even if I'm not someone else's favorite person, I will be my own.

Chapter 56

A Generation Of Drug Abuse

My mother was a great mother before she started drinking. We had mommy-daughter days where we'd get our hair or nails done together. We'd look in photo albums at old pictures of me, and we'd bake cookies.

My father was often in jail or in trouble, so I never looked at him for anything. My stepfather came into our lives when I was 4. I was never fond of my stepfather coming in and acting as if he were my dad—but he did a better job than my father.

When I was 7 or 8, my mom started going into the bathroom with a drink and her cigarettes. It seemed like she was trying to escape from something, and there was no telling who she would be coming out.

Sometimes she'd go in mean and come out calm, or she'd go in mean and come out worse. Sometimes, she got so drunk she couldn't pronounce her words.

I felt sad and upset every time she got like that. Worrying about how she'd be, my hands felt sweaty, my heart raced, and my body felt wobbly.

I now know that feeling is anxiety, and I've felt it ever since my mom started drinking.

My stepfather didn't drink, and when my mother did, he looked at her with disgust. They'd often fight once she got drunk.

When my mother was sober, she had all the power; she had a voice. But when she was drunk, he had the power and the voice.

Starting when I was 8 or so, their yelling turned into physical fighting.

No matter how much I disliked my mother drunk, I tried to stop my stepfather from putting his hands on her. When they fought, I would come in the room and yell at the top of my lungs, "STOP IT NOW! ENOUGH IS ENOUGH!"

I'm the oldest, seven years older than my little sister and nine years older than my brother. I tried to protect them from the drinking and especially the physical fighting. I was also trying to protect my mother.

Sometimes they'd stop fighting when I'd yell, but other times I couldn't do anything. My stepfather never hit me.

One time, when I was 10 and my little brother was only a few months old, they came home late from a party, her drunk and him angry.

I was woken up by screaming and crying. I got out of my bed, went down the hall, and saw my mother crying loudly and holding her ear, which was bleeding.

"What happened?" I asked.

My mother pointed to the closed front door. I opened the door and saw my brother's stroller turned over near the elevators with my brother lying on the floor nearby crying.

I was furious. Who in their right mind would do this to a baby? After I got my crying brother back in his stroller, I asked my mom what happened. She was crying and trying to talk: "He … hit … me in my face." Blood dripped through her hand onto the floor.

I took my brother, who was OK, to his room and ran back to help my mom. I yelled at my stepfather, "WHY? Why did you put your hands on my mother? Do you see her ear?"

"She was being disrespectful, so I slapped her," he said. I called the police.

They came 25 minutes later, and my mom told them it was a mistake. She didn't want Child Protective Services (CPS) to take her kids.

Even though I tried to protect my mom, she still abused me when she was drinking. It felt like she was letting her anger at my stepfather out on me.

Once she grabbed me by my hair and swung me from left to right like a jump rope. I could feel every strand of hair loosen from my scalp.

Grandma's Was a Haven

I spent most of my time at my grandma's house in Harlem. She and Grandpa and I watched TV and ate junk food. My grandma didn't drink or do drugs and that was nice. But my mom told me that it wasn't always that way. My grandmother was a different person before I was born.

My mother told me that my grandmother was on drugs for most of my mom's childhood. She neglected (but didn't abuse) my mom and her little brother, my Uncle Shawn. I was the first grandchild, and my grandma got sober after I was born.

My mom's abuse hit a new high one day when I was 12.

I came home late and my mother threw her hands up like a boxer. "Come on. Fight me," she said. I was confused.

Even though she regularly beat me, I thought, "Mothers don't fight their children like that." She hit me in the face over and over.

I felt like I had no choice but to defend myself. So I did it. I punched my mother.

As we fought, my stepfather reached in and grabbed my phone out of my pocket. In bed that night I planned to steal my phone back and then tell someone at school about the abuse.

Family Secrets

The next day, I told the school counselor. He asked me who I could stay with. I told him my grandma. He told me to go to her after school and stay with her so things could calm down at home.

But when I got to my grandmother's house, she said sadly, "You can't stay here. There's not enough space in this one-room studio for me, you, and Grandpa." So, she called CPS.

I later learned from CPS that even if there was room, I couldn't live with my grandmother because she had a criminal record.

She had shoplifted to feed my mom and uncle while she was on drugs. I was surprised when I learned that my grandma had been arrested. It really lowered my image of her.

I was placed in a group home while they found me a foster family. When I got to my foster mom's house, I thought, "It's nice," but I didn't want to be there. I wanted to be with my grandma.

While I was in care, my mom and I had to go to therapy; we had some sessions separately and others together.

Our therapist wanted to get down to the root of the pain and anger on both sides. At first, being in therapy wasn't my cup of tea. I didn't like talking to people I didn't know.

But once I started to talk to the therapist more, I started to really like her. Being able to talk to someone and not be judged or yelled at was the best.

In our sessions together, the therapist helped my mother and me talk and listen to each other.

In these sessions, I learned that my mother had been neglected by her mother. She inflicted so much pain on me because she never learned how to be loving and caring from her mom until she was an adult.

In therapy, I was also able to communicate that I was a sensitive child and that her yelling made me anxious.

After that, my mom tried harder to bring her voice down when she was loud with me.

Knowing that she was an abused child, not a monster, helped me feel safer crying in front of her, and she learned to respond kindlier to my tears.

When I was 14, after two years in foster homes, I was placed back home with my mother. She had cut way back on her drinking and was more of a mom and less of a crazy person. She and my stepfather didn't argue or fight anymore, and she no longer hit me.

I was happy to be back with her, but scared and anxious about her recovery. She went to a several-day rehab and that seemed to help. She came home with more confidence. I felt like this was a start of a great opportunity for her.

But I didn't feel welcomed back from foster care. My mother had many rules, while in foster care I did what I wanted. She put me to work doing most of the chores and was strict.

More Addiction

When I was 16, a friend gave me weed for the first time, and it eased my anxiety. When I was sad, weed made me happier and less fearful.

Soon I was doing it every day. My mother sat me down and said, "You are much more than weed. You can do so much in life."

She was right, and it hurt to let her down. I wasn't going to school, I stopped working, and I didn't respect myself like I used to. I didn't care how I looked. I wore the same clothes over and over.

Last year, my mom kicked me out of her house because I was coming home high every day. Maybe she saw herself in my addiction. She also saw her own mother, who was an addict up until my birth.

Soon after I moved out, my grandma died, which broke my heart. Mourning Grandma briefly brought my mom and me closer. I still miss my grandma, who accepted me and didn't judge me for getting high. She said, "I was young once."

I moved in with my girlfriend's family and we still live there. We want to get our own place; I'm 18 now and not in foster care.

I have been getting high regularly for two years, and my mom has been sober for four years. I call her or visit every weekend.

She tells me to stay focused and gives me advice about school and work. Sometimes she nags me about smoking, and it gets on my nerves, but I still feel proud of her for getting sober.

She has tried to help me with my addiction. She took me to an NA (Narcotics Anonymous) meeting for children of alcoholics and regular NA meetings for myself.

Seeing situations from other people's point of view was helpful. I understand now that I smoke to calm my anxiety.

Some of my anxiety came from school. Twice now I've failed to graduate from high school. Each time, the closer I got to graduation, the more my anxiety increased. I ended up dropping out.

But then I realized that I really wanted to pursue my dreams and I couldn't do that without my diploma.

So, I put myself back into a special high school that offers classes at night. I attend regularly and I don't smoke before school because it throws off my focus.

But I get high every day after school and spend about $20 a week on weed. With that money, I could get training for the career I want, doing hair and nails.

I know I should stop. If I could control the anxiety some other way, I would stop smoking.

Talking about my feelings helps me from needing to get high, but I've never talked to a therapist about weed because I worry, I'll get in trouble.

Other things that ease my anxiety are listening to music, writing in my journal, and writing songs.

Succeeding at things helps too: Feeling self-confident helps ease my anxiety, and I hope that when I get my diploma, it'll be easier to stop.

I've seen meetings help my mom, so I may go to an Alateen or Al-Anon meeting, which are support groups for people who have a loved one with a drinking problem, "Something You Can't Fix", I noticed that my mom is more confident since she got sober.

Because I don't have kids, addiction has had different effects on me than it did on previous generations.

My mom and grandma were abusive or neglectful to their children.

When I'm high, I mostly isolate myself. Weed is my safe place where I'm not hurting anyone. The only person I hurt, so far, is me.

Chapter 57

Child's worst Nightmare

A 16-year-old girl told the Sex Crime Unit of the New York City Police Department the so many times her dad raped her…

Everything started when Madelene was 14. She couldn't take it. She decided to go to the police.

The officers gathered all the information from Madelene. She was a rape victim.

The abuse began when her father started touching the sensitive parts of her body.

She told her brother about her father. She also said that she moved away from him. Madelene told her twin brother about it every day, but he ignored her and did not believe her.

The next day, he had sex me. He continued to do it after we moved. We were relocated so many times that I lost track of my address. I knew it was Palm Beach. That is all I know.

My father once had issues with his mistress, so he woke me up in the middle of the night. He took me into the guest room to sleep with me. He told me not to make any sound because he threatened to kill me. That is the reason I could not tell my mother.

She noticed many times that her father was acting strange. He was always claiming that their neighbors were interfering with their lives. He took her and her sibling to Florida, where he continued to harm her.

In Florida, it was not any different. There were many interventions of the landlord and other neighbors.

One day as I was doing my house shores, I heard a noise in the back yard. I opened the door. It was my father. He immediately took my bag and dragged me out. I started shouting for help...

Some boys came out and asked him where he was taking me.

He replied that she's my father and I would do whatever I please.

The landlord called the police. It was then I explained to the police that father had been having sex with me for almost two years. I also explained that my mother had no idea of all those incidents.

My mother was so upset when she found out that she made the decision on moving back to New York City. She didn't pressed charges against my dad. She told me that family affairs should be kept a secret.

When we returned to New York, I couldn't sleep. I kept thinking that my dad will return and start abusing me once again. I didn't tell my teacher because I was afraid to say anything.

Chapter 58

The Role of Educators

Children and adolescents spend a large portion of their time in school. This gives educators more time than any other professional to see the student behavior.

Keep in mind that the term "educator" is not only the classroom teachers. It means anyone that works closely within the school.

What I am trying to say, other school personnel involved in serving the child.

The primary goal of the education system is to teach. To achieve this, it is sometimes necessary to remove barriers that impede the child's ability to learn.

Educators are trained to recognize and intervene when a child is not able concentrate in class.

In the face of discouraging and overwhelming facts about child abuse and neglect, teachers should not only report cases of child abuse, but also help children become strong.

Can schools provide a refuge for children who are hurt and neglected at home?

I know the can, I teach a course in child abuse issues, for teachers renewing or seeking certification.

Agreeing to such an assignment meant wrestling with my own history and giving back to other teachers what a progression of good teachers gave me.

It meant asking already overburdened teachers to share my conviction that confronting the enormous waste and havoc of abusive relationships, and in particular their effects on the children we teach, is the right thing to do. It is also within our power.

Teachers come to my class already discouraged about the topic of child abuse. They don't need to be told that of every six cases of abuse reported to authorities, only one will receive more than passing attention. They can already guess that, for every six cases reported, 18 went unreported.

Some of my students say they are expecting to gain nothing from the course but a deepened sense of helplessness. Most have tried at least once to intercede on behalf of an abused child, only to be stonewalled or taken lightly.

Recent studies suggest that two-thirds of teacher-initiated reports may still go no farther than the principal's desk.

What can I teach people who already believe there is not much point in trying? First, we look at statistics and case histories that demonstrate the enormity and breadth of a devastating social problem that crosses socioeconomic and cultural groups.

Then we learn what to look for, what to say to the disclosing child, when and how to report to the authorities. Then I must tell the teachers that more than two-thirds of the children who desperately need help are masquerading as normal so convincingly that their abuse will go completely undetected.

We share stories about agonizingly slow responses from overwhelmed social service agencies. We hold up to the light some shameful skeletons in public education's own closet: A coach has an affair with a girl in his charge. A principal administers whacks with a paddle.

A sarcastic teacher undermines a student's already fragile sense of self. We note that these things still happen with appalling regularity.

After a couple of hours of this, most students wish they were home in front of the fire or playing with their own kids.

What keeps me offering the class is a hope that I can engender some optimism and new resolve. It's not that I believe that teachers, even teachers united, can solve the problem, or that reporting suspected child abuse always leads to an improved situation for the child, or that it's possible to intervene in every case.

But teachers can make a huge difference. Teachers can provide an effective counterbalance to the effects of an abusive home. It does not require special heroism. My challenge is to help teachers persevere, to keep their hope alive, by focusing on children's capacity for strength and how we can promote it.

Chapter 59

Enrich your Knowledge

Signs of a Dysfunctional Family

Unhealthy parenting signs, which could lead to a family becoming dysfunctional include:

Emotional intolerance family members are not allowed to express the "wrong" emotions.

Social dysfunction or isolation for example, parents unwilling to reach out to other families—especially those with children of the same gender and approximate age or do nothing to help their "friendless" child.

Stifled speech children not allowed to dissent or question authority.

Denial of "inner life" children are not allowed to develop their own value systems.

Being under- or over-protective

Apathy "I don't care!"

Belittling "You can't do anything right!"

Shame -"Shame on you!"

Bitterness regardless of what is said, using a bitter tone of voice.

Hypocrisy, "Do as I say, not as I do."

Lack of forgiveness for minor misdeeds or accidents

Judgmental statements or demonization, "You are a liar!"

Being overly critical and withholding proper praise. Experts say 80–90% praise, and 10–20% constructive criticism is the healthiest.

Double standards or giving "mixed messages" by having a dual system of values i.e., one set for the outside world, another when in private, or teaching divergent values to each child.

The absentee parent seldom available for their child due to work overload, alcohol/drug abuse, gambling, or other addictions.

Unfulfilled projects, activities, and promises affect children." We'll do it later."

Giving to one child what rightly belongs to another

Gender prejudice treats one gender of children fairly: the other unfairly.

Discussion and exposure to sexuality: either too much, too soon or too little, too late

Faulty discipline is based more on emotions or family politics than on established rules, e.g., punishment by "surprise".

Having an unpredictable emotional state due to substance abuse, personality disorder(s), or stress.

Parents always or never take their children's side when others report acts of misbehavior, or teachers report problems at school.

Scapegoating knowingly or recklessly blaming one child for the misdeeds of another.

"Tunnel vision" diagnosis of children's problems, for example, a parent may think their child is either lazy or has learning disabilities after he falls behind in school despite recent absence due to illness.

Older siblings give either no or excessive authority over younger siblings with respect to their age difference and level of maturity.

Frequent withholding of consent "blessing" for culturally common, lawful, and age-appropriate activities a child wants to take part in the "know-it-all" has no need to obtain the child's side of the story when accusing or listening to child's opinions on matters which greatly impact them.

Regularly forcing children to attend activities for which they are extremely over- or under-qualified (e.g., using a preschool to babysit a typical nine-year-old boy, taking a young child to poker games, etc.

Either being a miser "scrooge" in totality or selectively allowing children's needs to go unmet e.g., a father will not buy a bicycle for his son because he wants to save money for retirement or "something important".

Disagreements about nature and nurture parents, often non-biological, blame common problems on child's heredity, when faulty parenting may be the actual cause.

"Children as pawns"

One common dysfunctional parental behavior is a parent's manipulation of a child to achieve some outcome adverse to the other parent's rights or interests.

Examples include verbal manipulation such as spreading gossip about the other parent. Communicating with the parent through the child.

In the process of exposing the child to the risks of the other parent's displeasure with that communication rather than doing so directly, try to obtain information through the child.

Spying, or causing the child to dislike the other parent, with insufficient or no concern for the damaging effects of the parent's behavior on the child is dangerous.

While many instances of such manipulation occur in shared custody situations that have resulted from separation or divorce, it can also take place in intact families, where it is known as triangulation.

"Using" destructively narcissistic parents who rule by fear and conditional love.

Abusing parents who use physical violence, or emotionally, or sexually abuse their children.

Perfectionist, fixating on order, prestige, power, or perfect appearances, while preventing their child from failing at anything.

Dogmatic or cult-like, harsh, and inflexible discipline, with children not allowed, within reason, to dissent, question authority, or develop their own value system.

Inequitable parenting, going to extremes for one child while continually ignoring the needs of another.

<u>Look at the references I wrote. They will give you additional information….</u>

References

1. Coffey, R. (in press). Unspeakable Truths and Happy Endings. Lutherville, Md.: SIDRAN Foundation. (http://www.access. digex.net/~sidran/).
2. Kidder, T. (1989). Among Schoolchildren. New York: Avon Books.
3. Miller, A. (1983). For Your Own Good: Hidden Cruelty in Child-Rearing and the Roots of Violence, translated by Hildegarde and Hunter Hannum. New York: Farrar, Straus, Giroux.
4. Myers, J.E.B., ed. (1994). The Backlash: Child Protection Under Fire. London: Sage Publications.
5. National Child Rights Alliance. (1997). (http://linux.hartford. edu/~jerry/ ncra.html).
6. Pool, C.R. (March 1997). "Maximizing Learning: A Conversation with Renate Nummela Caine." Educational Leadership 54, 6: 11-15.
7. Rush, F. (1980). The Best Kept Secret. New York: McGraw-Hill.
8. Real Cédula de 1789 "para el comercio de Negros"
9. Rouse, Irving. The Tainos: Rise and Decline of the People Who Greeted Columbus ISBN 0-300-05696-6.
10. Mahaffy, Cheryl (January 28, 2006). "Vieques Island - What lies beneath". Edmonton Journal. Retrieved February 11, 2006.
11. Figueroa, Ivonne (July 1996). "Taínos". Retrieved March 20, 2006.

12. Pedro Torres. "The Dictionary of the Taíno Language". Taino Inter-Tribal Council Inc. Retrieved February 11, 2006.

13. Brau, Salvador (1894). Puerto Rico y su historia: investigaciones críticas (in Spanish). Valencia, Spain: Francisco Vives Moras. pp. 96–97.

14. Vicente Yañez Pinzón is considered the first appointed governor of Puerto Rico, but he never arrived on the island.

15. PROCLAMATION presented by Dennis O. Freytes, MPA, MHR, BBA, Chair/Facilitator, 500TH Florida Discovery Council Round Table, American Veteran, Community Servant, VP NAUS SE Region; Chair Hispanic Achievers Grant Council

16. Mari, Brenda A. (April 22, 2005). "The Legacy of Añasco: Where the Gods Come to Die". Puerto Rico Herald. Archived from the original on April 27, 2006. Retrieved March 1, 2006.

17. "Taino Tribal Census Registration: A Record of Hope and Survival-al". La Salita Cafe. Retrieved 28 November 2014.

18. Jones, W.A. "Porto Rico". Catholic Encyclopedia. Retrieved March 4, 2006.

19. "Religion". Puerto Rico: A Guide to the Island of Boriquén. Feder-al Writers Project. 1940. Retrieved March 6, 2006.

20. Hispanic Firsts, by, Nicolas Kanellos, publisher Visible Ink Press; ISBN 0-7876-0519-0; p.40

21. "La Fortaleza/San Juan National Historic Site, Puerto Rico". National Park Service. Archived from the original on February 8, 2006. Retrieved March 1, 2006.

22. Miller, Paul G. (1947).Historias de Puerto Rico,221–237.

23. "The Life of Sir Francis Drake". July 20, 2004. Retrieved March 1, 2006.

24. The exact number of ships and troops is presently uncertain. The number of ships varies from 60 to 64 ships and the number of troops varies from 7,000 to 13,000. No exact number of ships is given by British accounts. For more information see Alonso,

María M., and The Eighteenth Century Caribbean & The British Attack on Puerto Rico in 1797 ISBN 1-881713-20-2.

25. Alonso, María M. "Chapter XIV - Abercromby's Siege" (PDF). The Eighteenth Century Caribbean & The British Attack on Puerto Rico in 1797. Retrieved February 28, 2006.

26. Caro Costas, Aida R. (1980). Antología de Lecturas de Historia de Puerto Rico (Siglos XV-XVIII), p. 467.

27. Abbad y Lasierra, Iñigo. Historia Geográfica, Civil y Política de Puerto Rico (in Spanish). S.l.: Univ of Puerto Rico Pr. ISBN 0-8477-0800-4.

28. Interview of Thomas Ellingwood Fortin, Producer, NEW ALBION PICTURES

29. Words from Pres. Ronald Reagan

30. "Aspectos politicos en Puerto Rico: 1765–1837" (in Spanish). Retrieved March 4, 2006.

31. 150th. Anniversary of the Foundation of Arroyo, Puerto Rico

32. NY/Latino Journal; Taking the PE Out of PRT; by: Rafael Merino Cortes; July 20, 2006

33. "Slave revolts in Puerto Rico: conspiracies and uprisings, 1795-1873"; by: Guillermo A. Baralt; Publisher Markus Wiener Publishers; ISBN 1-55876-463-1, ISBN 978-1-55876-463-7

34. Grose, Howard B., Advance in the Antilles; the new era in Cuba and Porto Rico, OCLC 1445643 (These clauses included that slaves were required to continue working for three more years and that the owners would be compensated 35 million pesetas per slave.)

35. Negroni, Héctor Andrés (1992). Historia militar de Puerto Rico (in Spanish). Societal Stately Quinto Centenario. ISBN 978-84-7844-138-9.

36. "Chronology of Puerto Rico in the Spanish-American War". Li-brary of Congress. Retrieved March 10, 2006.

37. This legislature consisted of a Council of Administration with eight elected and seven appointed members, and a Chamber

of Rep-resentatives with one member for every 25,000 inhabitants.

38. Strategy as Politics by Jorge Rodriguez Beruff; Publisher: La Editorial; Universidad de Puerto Rico; page 7; ISBN 978-0-8477-0160-5

39. "The World of 1898: The Spanish-American War". Hispanic Division, Library of Congress. Retrieved 2008-08-03.

40. "Military Government in Puerto Rico". Library of Congress. Retrieved March 26, 2006.

41. Blackburn Moreno, Ronald (February 2001). "Brief Chronology of Puerto Rico" (PDF). ASPIRA Association, Inc. Archived from the original (PDF) on February 17, 2006. Retrieved February 11, 2006.

42. My aunt Luz E. Pagan Rodriguez,
My uncle Ramon L. Pagan Rodriguez
My father Juan J. Pagan Rodriguez
My Grandmother Ceferina Figueroa Bello
My Grandmother Guadalupe Rodriguez Quiles
Told me many stories about Puerto Rico
& my FAMILY

43. A Loving Approach to Dementia Care: Making Meaningful Connections with the Person Who Has Alzheimer... by Laura Wayman

44. The 36-Hour Day: A Family Guide to Caring for People Who Have Alzheimer Disease, Related Dementias... by Nancy L. Mace

45. Creating Moments of Joy for the Person with Alzheimer's or Dementia: A Journal for Caregivers, Fourth Edition by Jolene Brackey

46. Learning to Speak Alzheimer's: A Groundbreaking Approach for Everyone Dealing with the Disease By Joanne Koenig Coste-

47. The 36-Hour Day: A Family Guide to Caring for People Who Have Alzheimer Disease, Related Dementias, and Memory Loss by Nancy L. Mace

48. Thoughtful Dementia Care: Understanding the Dementia Experience by Jennifer Ghent-Fuller

49. Activities to do with Your Parent who has Alzheimer's Dementia by Judith A. Levy EdM...

50. An Unintended Journey: A Caregiver's Guide to Dementia by Ja-net Yagoda Shagam

51. How to Help Your Friend with Cancer
By Colleen Fulbright

52. Breast Cancer Journey The Essential Guide to Treatment and Recovery Edited by Ruth O'Regan, edited by Sheryl G. A. Gabram, Edited by Terri Ades, Edited by Rick Alteri, edited by Joan L. Kramer, Edited by Kimberly A. Stump-Sutliff

53. My Cancer Days
By Courtney Filigenzi, Illustrated by Nicole

Norma Iris Pagan Morales was born in Ponce, Puerto Rico. She comes from a very lovable family. Her parents, Juan Jose Pagan Rodriguez, and Digna Morales Figueroa, now deceased, always helped her with her projects as a writer and teaching career.

Norma had three siblings, Adelin Milagros Pagan Morales, Juan Jose Pagan Morales, and Julio Manuel Pagan Morales. Julio Manuel Pagan Morales died on September 19, 1998, and my dear sister Adelin Milagros Pagan Morales died on February 17, 2023.

Norma did all her academic studies in New York City, Puerto Rico, and Canada. She worked in the City of New York Police Department. As an Educator, she worked in New York City Bd. of Education as an English Teacher, in Puerto Rico Bd. of Education as an English teacher and in the Puerto Rico Army National.

She has teaching certifications for English as a Second Language and Teaching English as a Foreign Language.

She had published fifteen books: Proud of My Puerto Rican Bequest, ¿Porque Soy Boricua? Poemas del Alma, Art in Written Form, A

Baffling Short Stories Collection, On Job in the Big Apple, Puerto Rican Soldiers Serving with Pride, Nature's Rage in the Caribbean, Boricua de Pura Cepa, You are the One, The Unfaithfuls, Christopher Columbus, Violence in the City, Poemas Tiernos and Mis Raices